Praise For
SHATTERED COMPASS

"*Shattered Compass* is both a coming-of-age story and a journey of redemption. Lenore Greiner probes a long-ago loss of innocence to exorcise ghosts that had haunted her for decades as she seeks her path to wholeness. On journeys far, wide, and within, she finds solace and arrives at peace. Her success provides hope for us all."

— **LARRY HABEGGER**, EXECUTIVE EDITOR, *TRAVELERS' TALES*

"In this bittersweet and deeply felt memoir, the heroine careens into womanhood, buffeted and victimized but also charmed and challenged, as she explores the Italian territory of her heritage. We see her first as an American student abroad, then as she builds a family in California. Finally, we join her decades later in Italy again, fighting to make peace with history and memory."

— **CHRISTOPHER REYNOLDS**, TRAVEL WRITER, *LOS ANGELES TIMES*

"The satisfaction in reading memoirs is often more than being transported by a compelling story and enthralled by good writing, it comes in discovering your own story within another person's telling. Such was my experience reading Lenore Greiner's new memoir. *Shattered Compass: A Memoir of Loss, Escape, and Renewal* tells a story of a young woman's pain, love, loss, and, ultimately, healing in a journey both inward and worldwide. Written with the generous detail of an experienced travel writer, this memoir will touch your heart and, perhaps, set you on the road toward your own discovery."

— **JUDY REEVES**, AUTHOR OF *WHEN YOUR HEART SAYS GO*

"*Shattered Compass* is a feat of vulnerability and strength. Lenore Greiner leads us along a path of transcendence as she chronicles her journey from innocence to disillusionment and finally to healing. This beautifully written memoir is a must-read!"

— **LESLIE FERGUSON**, AWARD-WINNING AUTHOR OF *WHEN I WAS HER DAUGHTER*

"Lenore Greiner's memoir, *Shattered Compass: A Memoir of Loss, Escape, and Renewal,* took me on a journey through her life and helped me to reflect on how one life event, when you are young, can color so many other future moments. She writes honestly about hardships and the challenging road of overcoming and healing from past experiences. She beautifully captures some of the mysteries of loss and the seemingly unreal encounters we can have when we are open to the thin veil that separates this life from the next. As a travel writer, she can't help but weave her various voyages abroad into the full picture of her life."

— **LEEANN BARTOLINI**, PHD., PROFESSOR OF PSYCHOLOGY, DOMINICAN UNIVERSITY OF CALIFORNIA

"*Shattered Compass* takes readers on an unforgettable journey through tragedy, love, and self-discovery, all set against breathtaking landscapes. At its heart, *Shattered Compass* explores the resilience of the human spirit— finding love in unexpected places, enduring heartbreaking loss, and uncovering profound lessons through the passage of time and the act of traveling.

Greiner's evocative prose immerses us in vivid settings both near and far, bringing each moment to life with lyrical beauty. More than a mere coming-of-age tale, *Shattered Compass* is a profound testament to the resilience of the human spirit and the transformative power of redemption, even when life's path is shrouded in uncertainty. This is a deeply moving and inspiring tale that reminds us to embrace the unexpected and trust in the healing power of the journey."

— **KRISTEN FOGLE**, EXECUTIVE DIRECTOR, SAN DIEGO WRITERS, INK

SHATTERED COMPASS

A Memoir of Loss, Escape, and Renewal

LENORE GREINER

*Helping talented writers
publish exceptional books.*

www.AcornPublishingLLC.com

For information, address:
Acorn Publishing, LLC
3943 Irvine Blvd. Ste. 218
Irvine, CA 92602

Shattered Compass: A Memoir of Loss, Escape, and Renewal

CITATION/CREDIT REFERENCE
A version of the chapter "My Father's Moon" first appeared in the International Memoir Writers Association Anthology What Just Happened? Shaking the Tree: brazen. short. memoir., ed. Marni Freedman and Tracy J. Jones, vol. 6, 2025.

Interior design and formatting by Debra Cranfield Kennedy

Printed in the United States of America

Library of Congress Control Number: 2024923060

ISBN-13: 979-8-88528-121-8 (paperback)

AUTHOR'S NOTE

This memoir is a nonfiction work based on my experiences, reflections, and recollections. I've tried to portray events as accurately as possible. Since memory is imperfect, I've recreated some details, timelines, and conversations to the best of my ability to ensure clarity and narrative flow.

To protect privacy, I've changed names and identifying details where necessary. Beyond these intentional changes, any resemblance to real persons, living or deceased, is purely coincidental.

This story is true and as I experienced it. Others may have their own perspectives; this book doesn't attempt to represent their stories.

*For Rob—a steadfast survivor who taught me
the true meaning of grace and strength.
This book, like our life, is richer because of you.*

*For my father, Leonard Caesar Asiano,
who lived a life of purpose, faith, and love–
plus a dash of adventure.*

1

INNOCENCE ADRIFT

I was nineteen years old and on my way to a palace.

Bundled up in a wool scarf and heavy coat, I walked to school in my red leather boots with a broken heel, pondering my life in Italy.

On an impulse, I entered the church to attend the service, though I'd be late for Italian class, and joined other celebrants in a wooden pew. The chilly and vast interior of the 530-year-old Gothic cathedral under towering marble and stone arches was magnificent. Studying the massive altar inside a vaulted nave illuminated by a morning sun pouring through stained-glass windows, I thought maybe I felt so sad because I never asked God for help.

I muffled my gravelly coughs, got down on my knees, and began to pray. Within the cavernous stone expanse, no answers came in the dim amid the worshippers' echoing voices. *Why did my life turn out like this, all alone and living with a wound impossible to heal?*

Hunched in the church's frigid air, I decided to skip Mass and left for school.

Later that day, I wrote a letter home in my student pension room. I longed for more compassion from my parents, but I could never reveal the ugly turn my life had taken over the past two months. Instead, I wrote about my misconception that Perugia was like my hometown of Mill Valley, California. "There are dangers," I wrote. "I want to be able to recognize the dangers."

I also noted, "I don't feel good, but I don't feel like giving up and coming back. There's too much to learn … about me or how I'd act in certain situations. I don't know whether this is clear or not. I hope you can see my meaning or what I've been through."

No one wrote back asking for clarification.

But my younger sister, Grace, picked up on something between the lines. In her letter, she wrote, "From your last letter to Mom, your tone seemed depressed about something. What is really going on with you? I really would like to know. Maybe I can help. Please tell me."

I never answered her question. I could never write down the words anyway.

Two months earlier, I had left home for the first time to attend the Università per Stranieri, the University for Foreigners, in Perugia. The plan was to study Italian, art, and culture for a year.

Free at last, I was learning to fly. But I didn't have wings.

Excited and nervous after landing in this Umbrian hill town, I was knocked by frustration. I couldn't speak enough Italian to navigate daily life. Snotty salesgirls rolled their eyes as I stammered and searched for the right words. In restaurants, waiters presented me with a horrific slab of liver or horsemeat, and my mouth twisted in disgust before gagging. *I didn't order that, did I?*

Grabbing my dictionary, I began memorizing as many words as possible.

Every day, things scrambled out of order. After opening a detergent bottle, the smell told me I had wasted money on bleach. The laundry I hung outside my window to dry in the morning became soaked by afternoon rains. I fought with ancient, poorly hung Italian doors and confusing locks, feeling lost and incompetent in a beautiful place.

Italy the infuriating. Though unacclimated to living on my own, I could easily forgive my ancestral country as the afternoon sun burnished ornate buildings into gold, as I ate luscious food, rambled along cobblestone streets, or joined the townsfolk on traffic-free Corso Vannucci.

On my first day of class, I squeezed past Fiats parked with great anarchy along Via Ulisse Rocchi. Rubbing my eyes, I had awakened too early that September morning and couldn't dress fast enough, my hands shaking with excitement.

Amid buzzing mopeds and the Italian language filling my ears, my new leather backpack banging against my back, I swung down the narrow passage. An espresso machine hissed in a nearby café, and my nose caught the intoxicating scent of a bakery.

I wanted to soak up every fabulous thing about my new Italian life. I marveled at the simplest details—a Fiat sign, a woman heaving her market basket, the bantering school kids. And I ached to share this beauty with everyone back home.

Suddenly, an Alfa Romeo squad car driven by a policeman zoomed too close, threatening to rub me against a rough stone wall. As I spun out of his way, my head just missed two dead rabbits hanging on hooks outside a butcher shop—an advertisement for today's fresh meat. I smiled and shrugged without a care.

Untouristed and authentic, Perugia hummed with the vibrant energy of two universities. Though the University of Perugia dates back to 1308 while my university was founded in 1921, medieval history permeated the whole city. At the University of Perugia, ten thousand students studied everything from engineering to art or attended vet school, law school, or medical school.

At the bottom of Via Ulisse Rocchi, I entered Piazza Fortebraccio through the Etruscan Gate, a thick stone arch that had stood for over two millennia. I walked faster toward an eighteenth-century Baroque palace, the Palazzo Gallenga, which housed my university.

Once inside, I ascended wide marble steps worn concave by centuries of feet to find my Italian language class in ornate Classroom Three. Underneath an embellished and frescoed ceiling, I joined French, Japanese, Spanish, Persian, Swedish, and Nigerian students at long eighteenth-century-style desks and benches in stepped-up rows like in a small theater.

Giddy with anticipation, I chose a seat underneath a Venetian glass chandelier. Listening to a babel of languages, I pulled out my pen and notebook and looked around to take in the red walls, gilded moldings, tall windows, and old paintings hung in heavy gold frames.

This is too much. What a place to learn Italian.

Before embarking on my adventure and leaving everything I knew behind, I imagined Italy as that captivating destination in travel magazines and movies—where Audrey Hepburn explored lively, sunlit streets in *Roman Holiday*. Unbeknownst to me or my parents, I had landed in a shadowy Italy during the seventies, an era the Italians call the anni oscuri, the dark years.

A year earlier, the Getty heir kidnapping and torture had created international headlines. Worse, months before I arrived, Palestinian terrorists had stormed Rome's airport, spraying the terminal with submachine fire and firebombing a Pan Am jet. They slaughtered thirty-four people. Afterward, travelers landing in Rome found Italian soldiers, Uzis in hand, on guard throughout the terminal.

2

FARFALLA

Before my classes began, my mother and I arrived to search for my student accommodation after checking into the eighteenth-century Hotel della Posta on Corso Vannucci. Stepping into our room, I entered a wondrous world of ceiling frescos and scrolled gilt work. I bounced on my bed, in awe of the lavish décor and antique armoires. Then, I hopped up and opened a window over Corso Vannucci, listening to the Italian conversations below and observing the locals on their afternoon strolls toward the Piazza IV Novembre. Every street and alley led to this main piazza; many descended from footpaths formed before Christ was born.

I felt like the whole world had opened up to me. *This is where I live now.*

I studied women parading in the latest Italian fashions, sumptuous furs, and fine footwear. They pushed strollers holding gorgeous babies or children cosseted in multi-colored knits and matching hats. Dressed as a typical Mill Valley girl, I felt sloppy in my jeans and silver hippie jewelry. Mom looked elegant in her skirt and heels, so I figured I must dress up more to fit in.

"This is not the room I paid for," Mom said. She grabbed the phone and informed the front desk, "We're supposed to have a larger room with a bathroom. And not over a noisy street."

What's wrong with this room? It's gorgeous. "Mom," I whispered. "It's okay."

"No, it's not, Lenore."

I felt embarrassed as Mom disregarded me. We traded this vibrant room with a city view for a quiet room with a bathroom.

The following day, we left the hotel lobby to check out the student housing. A bit older than me, an elegant woman sat perched at the hotel bar, sipping coffee. I tilted my head, curious about her. Sylph-like and graceful, she had long strawberry-blond hair that tumbled down her back.

I remembered she'd been there when we checked in the night before. Why was she there again?

When we returned in the afternoon, she sat alone, sipping wine patiently, waiting. But for what?

And when we returned from dinner, there she was, wearing an exquisite, long, green silk gown.

Did she live in the hotel? What was she waiting for?

After two days of this chic tableau, I approached the desk clerk and said, "Excuse me, Sir, but why is that woman always in your bar?"

"Why, she is the house girl," replied the hotelman, all business. "Her name is Farfalla."

Butterfly. Farfalla's pure beauty shocked me. She looked nothing like the trashy-looking prostitutes I'd seen in movies.

In my guidebook, I read how Italian hotels offered their house girls like fine wine. Clerks asked lone men if they needed an extra blanket. If so, a girl would be right up. I also learned and appreciated the Italians' poetic

At sixteen, I enjoyed a rare silent moment with my family at our Tahoe cabin.
Image courtesy of the author's collection.

nickname for prostitutes: lucciole—fireflies. Fireflies burn bright at night. Italian law allowed fireflies to work privately, permitting loitering yet outlawing streetwalking. How the police made the distinction puzzled me.

I sure wasn't in Mill Valley anymore.

We toured several student pensions, simple rooms with shared baths in an apartment or house. We found my new place near school. It was a bare room with a single bed, an armoire, a desk, and a chair. Hot water was available twice weekly for bathing and laundry, but heating oil cost extra.

I twirled around in my new abode. "This sure is different from living in a big house with a noisy family," I told Mom.

I didn't tell her it was also very quiet, perhaps too quiet.

After I settled in, Mom got busy shopping for gifts back home, covering every local boutique, shop, and department in the Standa retail store. Impatient, I jiggled while waiting for her.

We passed cafés full of students, kids my age having fun without parents. I turned around to look at them, burning with jealousy. Glaring with irritation at Mom, I wondered when she'd leave so I could start my new life. *Longest three days ever. Jesus.*

In the Covered Market, I lost her amid vegetable sellers, kitchenware, and Italian fashions. I sat in a little café with an espresso, put my chin into my palm, and thought about how this all had started as Mom's idea.

One evening last winter, Mom walked into the bedroom I shared with my little sister, Grace, as we did homework. She handed me an article about the University for Foreigners and asked, "Do you think you'd be interested in this?"

"Maybe." I took the article with shaky hands, my eyes growing wide. Grace looked stunned.

I read that tuition cost only fifteen dollars a quarter and student room and board under a hundred dollars a month—unheard of even in the seventies. But the deal was that I'd have to work and save money to pay for extra expenses such as traveling.

As her shocking idea sank in, I thought, *Wow, a year in Italy could help me become a good writer.* I loved reading works by Hemingway, Fitzgerald, and other members of the Lost Generation. I imagined myself as a brilliant expat, writing about life abroad.

But what about Jackson?

My boyfriend Jackson lived across the bay, studying at UC Berkeley. With my excellent grades at the College of Marin, I'd qualified for entrance there the following September.

Thinking about the same thing, Grace asked about Jackson as soon as Mom left our room.

"Hmm, well," I said as I brushed lint off the leg of my jeans, "it's only for a year—no big deal. We'll be together at Berkeley when I get back. We're never going to break up."

"Remember," said Grace, "when the Bianchis sent Simonetta to that convent school in Florence during her sophomore year? You know, 'to straighten her out,' as they said?"

"Yeah, I do. Wow, is that why they want to ship me off for a year abroad? Do I need straightening out?" Perhaps the Asiano authorities, as Jackson called my parents, hated the idea of me living near him across the Bay, beyond their control.

Mom and Dad had watched us grow close over the past year and a half, afraid we were having sex. And so what if we were?

Very accustomed to Mom's disappearances when shopping, I sipped my espresso more slowly, listening for her tinkling gold bracelets.

I spotted her in a shoe seller's booth.

"I found these, Lenore," she said, holding a pair of creamy red Italian leather boots. "Try them on."

I pulled them on; they looked so cool. "Wow, I love them! Thank you!"

As Mom paid the vendor, I bent to study my boots. They matched my upbeat mood and added a silver lining to my dream Italian life. They would help me and my Mill Valley jeans fit in better.

Finally, my new life began two days later when Mom left to meet Dad in Madrid. The three of us made a plan to meet in Rome a couple weeks later for our last weekend together, sightseeing, dining, and shopping.

Waiting with Dad for Mom outside a shop, we watched the stunning

Roman women and their fascinating sidewalk fashion show. Moving gracefully and tossing their long hair, they wore oversized sunglasses, gold chains, and well-cut coats.

Later, Dad couldn't help remarking to our hotel clerk, "Italian women are so beautiful."

"But Signore," he replied, placing his hand over his heart, "all women are beautiful."

Dad and I rode a bus early Sunday morning to the Vatican Museum; Mom preferred sleeping in. Through the bus window, I saw lone women standing on deserted street corners and looking expectantly at passing cars and pedestrians.

Oh my God, are they still working from the night before?

Unfortunately, I had to ask my father a question that I never would've dreamed of asking. "Are they prostitutes, Dad?"

"Well, yeah," said the former Naval officer who had circumnavigated the globe. "They need money for the collection basket at Mass, too, Lenore."

That evening, after dinner, we fended off another species of firefly. Walking back to our hotel in the dark, a group of tall, beautifully made-up high-fashion models materialized on the sidewalk, their sparkly evening gowns gleaming in the night.

When they swaggered with aggression toward Dad, I recognized this gaggle as male sex workers. Supremely gorgeous male sex workers. They drew near, enticing my father for an invitation to his hotel room. Ever the seasoned international traveler, Dad ignored them.

I yelled at them. "Vai via—go away!" But secretly, my curiosity about legal Italian prostitution grew. I obsessed over Farfalla and *fireflies,* the human kind.

The next day, while shopping with Mom, I browsed around an English bookstore on Via Nazionale and made a serendipitous discovery: an English book on the history of Italian prostitution. What a find! I devoured it on the train back to Perugia.

The ancient Romans neither stigmatized nor outlawed prostitution and only required registration. For an easy income, even upper-class women practiced the trade. If a lower-class woman couldn't afford to register, she was branded as a prostibula. *So that's where we got the word "prostitute." Very cool.*

Prostitutes of both sexes lurked in the shadows underneath the fornices, or arches, of Roman buildings. That's where we got the word "fornication." A firefly might offer many specialties, including serving her clients as a fellatrix. Yes, both "fellatrix" and "fellatio" come from the Latin verb "fellare," which means "to suck."

Even more astonishing, I read that the Romans venerated a prostitute goddess, the mythical, wealthy, and notorious Acca Larentia. Every December 23rd, Romans celebrated her during an annual Larentalia festival, which some historians date back to sixth century BCE. Later, the Holy Roman Catholic Church replaced this pagan festivity with Christian holy days.

I closed my book. *Is a prostitute the reason we celebrate Christmas in December?*

I stared out the train window. So the Catholic Church sanitized that tradition and reshaped it into Christmas, just like the temples of Venus were reshaped into Christian basilicas over the centuries.

At nineteen, I hungered for the stories that had been rewritten or buried. I wanted to understand how things truly were and learn what had been softened and made more palatable.

The past had always fascinated me—not only historically but also personally. What else did the world rewrite? And what did it mean to desire something? To own one's body, one's pleasure? I was at an age where

I came to Italy for a year to become a writer. Instead, that year became about survival.
Image courtesy of the author's collection.

these weren't just abstract questions. I was in Italy, a country where sensuality seemed as natural as breathing, where beauty was celebrated without shame. I was watching the way the culture moved—how legal prostitution still existed, how the Italians accepted that desire, in all its forms, as a simple part of life.

I wasn't sure what I was searching for. Maybe I wanted to understand something about myself before I even knew the question I was asking. What did I want? What was I allowed to want?

I didn't know then how soon these questions would no longer feel like a choice, when my own body would transform into a battlefield.

And I didn't know that soon, silence would feel like my only choice. The world's demand for the "clean" story would weigh on me so heavily that I'd try to rewrite my own—into something acceptable, something survivable.

But at nineteen, before all of that, I was just curious about how history twists itself into new shapes, how societies justify what they once embraced, all behind the thin veil between the sacred and the profane. And maybe, in some quiet way, I was also trying to understand the kind of story I was about to step into myself.

3

ITALY IN AGONY

One day, during lunch break, two new friends, Austrian guys from the Tyrol, asked me to go with them to the student cafeteria.

We hiked down a steep street to the Italian university's cafeteria to join the crowded tables buzzing with students. The enticing aroma of fresh-baked bread wafting into my nostrils made me ravenous. Other classmates joined us: lanky Peter from Switzerland and bubbly Moppy from Argentina. I was Lenore from California. That's how we introduced ourselves.

"My landlady is a real bitch," said Peter from Switzerland, twirling his pasta on a fork. "I spoke French to a friend, and she said, 'You shouldn't speak English but Italian.' And she won't allow any girls in my room."

During our espresso-fueled banter, I studied the Italian students in the dining hall, especially the beautiful young Italian men. As I stuffed myself with pizza that made me swoon, I noticed a Persian guy reading a University of Colorado Boulder brochure with the Rockies on the cover. He said, "I want to study here, in the US."

"I know Persian students back in San Francisco who got free US college educations from the Shah. Why not you?"

He shook his head. "I don't like Shah. He keeps all the money to himself and puts it in a Swiss bank."

Gosh, I'm in a new world. Not just an Italian world but an international *one.*

After a long day of freedom, I walked home through a medieval maze of passageways and got lost, my map useless. Narrow, winding lanes transformed into unexpected stairways or ended at tall stone walls. Others opened onto small piazzas only to close up again.

I didn't care. I just retraced my steps, almost skipping home in my new red boots, chuckling to myself how it might take a whole year to find my way around.

In my pension room, I sat at a little wooden desk, happy to untangle Italian verbs and drill myself on passato remoto, a past tense for the distant past.

I repeated, "Abbi, avesti, ebbe, avemmo, aveste, ebbero."

Below my window, drunken boys stumbled by in the night, singing.

Just as they'd done in Romeo and Juliet's time.

Wracked with homesickness by bedtime, I picked up a pen with a sigh and wrote a cheery letter home detailing my new life:

> Ciao Mama,
>
> I'm having fun. Anyways, last night, I introduced my American friends, Missy, Vicky, and Ann, to three of my Italian friends, Paolo, Matteo, and Gian-Carlo, and you'd think I opened the gates of heaven for them. They all got along, and we had lots of fun.
>
> The weather changes. Yesterday, it drizzled and was very cold.
>
> I got letters from Jackson, Marie, and Ellie. It's good to hear how things are in Mill Valley, but it

seems so unreal! It was like a dream as if Mill Valley
had never existed.

Tell Dad I love him, and Banco di Roma sends its
regards.

Ciao,

L.

A big kiss to Dad, Grace, Angelo, Ricci, and Leo!

Then, I wrote to Jackson, the boyfriend I left behind, "I'm living in a twenty-four-hour foreign movie. I'm here—I can't believe it!"

I hardly missed him those first heady weeks.

He wrote back from his Berkeley dorm, "Write soon. Because I miss you very much, and I love you. Send me a picture of yourself so I can remember what you look like."

Did I send him my picture? Or did Italy distract me too much?

One October afternoon after class, I headed to the piazza for errands to find jammed traffic, roaming goat and sheep herds, and idling tractors. A mixture of animal dung, engine fumes, and cheap cigarettes stung my nose amid the espresso aromas from cafés. Local farmers had stormed the Piazza IV Novembre, striking against trade practices. At a newsstand, I read *TIME* magazine's international edition headline: "Italy In Agony." The Italian government had just collapsed amid soaring oil prices. No wonder my land-lady charged me extra for heating oil.

But it wasn't a big deal. I wasn't an Italian citizen, so it wouldn't affect me.

I entered a pharmacy and confronted Italy's mysterious coin shortage. After paying for supplies with a 500-lire bill, the cashier placed a coin, a stick of gum, and a rubber band in my palm for my change.

"No, no. Money, please," I said, stumbling over my Italian words.

She shook her head. "There isn't any."

In defeat, I headed up Corso Vannucci to Banco di Roma, unaware I was about to become a casualty of Italy's labyrinthine banking system despite Dad strolling up California Street in San Francisco and making his monthly deposit into our account.

After I requested my monthly withdrawal inside the busy branch, my teller shook his head and said, "There isn't any."

I stammered in baby Italian, "But it take one day to come. I come here two times to get money."

He shrugged in response, and my frustration overtook me. "Why Banco di Roma so bad?"

"Who can say?" he answered.

As profound fear carved into my gut, I stepped outside my bank to figure out how to pay rent. And buy food. I could write home about my late money, but with Italy's sluggish postal service, my letters took weeks to arrive. Transcontinental phone calls and cables cost too much, and I didn't have the money anyway, damn it.

Peter from Switzerland strolled by.

"Lenore, how are you?"

I managed a panicked smile. "I'm great." I felt anything but great. I looked up and down the street, confused. I had to figure out something for dinner soon. Then, I'd try the bank tomorrow. That evening, in the land of the world's most renowned cuisine, I chewed day-old bread in front of a bakery window displaying delicacies of unimaginable transcendence.

Walking home, I stumbled on the uneven pavement in my red boots, breaking a heel.

"God damn it," I muttered. *Now I've got to pay for a repair, and I don't have the money.*

In our class, I befriended Missy from Maryland, who had bouncy, sun-streaked curls and became a bright spot in my loneliness.

One afternoon, I ran into her as she walked quickly down Corso Vannucci, and I asked, "Where are you going?"

"To the Brufani Palace," Missy said as she kept walking.

Perugia's fanciest hotel where students never darkened its elegant marble entry? "How come?"

"Well, we need toilet paper," she said.

"From the hotel?" Ingenious.

As casually as possible, I followed her into a lobby adorned with crystal chandeliers under a glass ceiling. We passed a crackling fireplace, and I longed to sink into the silk-upholstered chair placed before it.

Missy led me into the lobby restroom, perhaps the finest in town.

I set my backpack down near a sink, saying, "It's so clean. And heated! Let's pee."

Afterward, squealing as I washed my hands in hot water, I said, "Oh my God, you know, my place only has hot water twice a week."

"Barbaric," said Missy, busy stuffing toilet paper rolls into our backpacks. "How do you do laundry or bathe enough?"

"Well, it's not easy."

"Look, you can take a bath at my place anytime."

"Oh, thanks. That's a nice offer," I said.

Feigning innocence, we walked outside. Then Missy took off running, and I caught up with her. We hugged, laughed, and celebrated our successful toilet paper scam.

She also showed me how to steal food, but that heist created too much drama. After lunch in the cafeteria, we passed the cheese and bread station. Without warning, Missy grabbed chunks of cheese and bread and stuffed everything down my V-neck sweater. She leaned over another counter and grabbed a bottle of San Pellegrino mineral water with one hand and pieces of fruit with another. She hid those under her coat.

Embroiled in her deception, I followed her to the exit without time to think.

"We're saving money on dinner tonight," she whispered in delight.

She had me at "saving money."

We followed a crowd of students to make our unsuspicious exit through two swinging glass doors. Due to poor timing, one door swung against Missy's glass bottle, shattering a door and spraying glass shards across the entrance.

"Shit!" I looked at Missy in shock.

She said one word: "Run."

She sped uphill into the maze of paths, ascending to the town center for a clean getaway.

I jumped when a cafeteria worker appeared, asking, "What happened?"

"I don't know." I walked away as carefree as possible, my feet crunching on the glass as I wondered how I was going to kill Missy.

I climbed up the piazza and found her hanging out on the cathedral steps. Without a word, I sat beside her, holding the cheese and bread.

"Let me make it up to you," she said. "Would you like to come to my program's Thanksgiving dinner next month—a real one with turkey and all the fixings?"

I eagerly said yes. That would save me money near the dreaded end of the month, and I'd get to celebrate a holiday on an ordinary Thursday in Italy.

The next morning, before class started, she sadly told me, "Our advisor said you can't come. Since, you know, because you're not in our program."

"You know that defeats the whole purpose of sharing a Thanksgiving feast."

"Yeah, sorry. No stray Americans allowed."

I slumped in my seat, feeling isolated, a lone wolf. Would it have been better to attend through a US university program as Missy did? She shared a sunny apartment with two other girls and had hot water daily. Was my suffering necessary? I had to remind myself that suffering in beautiful Italy hardly seemed like suffering.

With central heating rare in medieval hill towns, a damp chill sank into my bones as autumn arrived.

Being in Italy alone without a supportive program, I spent dark and cold evenings alone in my silent room, which intensified my homesickness.

One evening, I found two letters from home lying on my desk. I snatched them and tore them open. I got under the covers of my bed to warm up while reading.

I laughed out loud, reading my sister Grace's letter. The inconvenient Mill Valley police kept picking her up for curfew violations. The final straw came when she sat in a car with two guys after a party, drinking their last beers at three a.m. Dad got so mad, she wrote, but mostly because he had to pick her up at the police station at four in the morning.

Dad had the last word, writing at the bottom of her letter, "Everything is fine. If we can keep your sister off the police blotter."

After my bank fiasco, more money trouble landed. One morning, my Italian teacher, Professoressa Franchini, who was probably in her late twenties but as gorgeous as a *Vogue Italia* model, passed out notices about tuition due for the winter quarter. And she instructed us on how to negotiate the tangle of Italian bureaucracy.

"First, go to the police station," she said, her long, wavy titian hair spilling over her tight burgundy sweater that matched her velvet jeans. "Bring your passport with your student visa stamp inside, your bank passbook, and your student ID card."

My stomach tightened—all this just to pay tuition? I'd never been inside an actual police station before. Feeling unsure why we had to go to the police station, I became uneasy. Whatever this was, it wasn't nothing.

"Pay the fee for a new student visa stamp, and then pay your tuition to the police. A total of 10,000 lire a month."

Pay my tuition to the police? How could I be sure they wouldn't pocket the cash?

"Then go to the school office," continued our professoressa, "and pick up your new student card and class schedule. Does everyone understand?"

I didn't fully understand. Why couldn't I pay my tuition at school after showing my new student visa? That seemed like the normal way to do things. Why couldn't Italy be easier to live in?

Groaning, I reached into my purse, pushing aside my useless "change" of caramels, rubber bands, and gum to count my meager stack of lire.

Back in my room, with an annoyed scowl, I began the unpleasant task of writing to my parents to ask for money. They were going to freak, but what other option did I have?

> The police want 10,000 lire a month, beginning in
> January, because that's how it is. I found out at
> school, and that's how it's done. NO, I'M NOT IN
> TROUBLE WITH THEM.

I added that last sentence to answer the first question Mom would ask.

Then, a volley of suspicious inquiries began as her express letters arrived daily. She wrote, "It seems awfully high. Did you get in some trouble—is this why they're making you pay?"

I shot off more details in my own express letter, only to receive this:

> We are all very concerned about that 10,000 lire you
> must pay the police of Perugia. You must have
> caused some problems for them to assess this fee. I
> have already written to the police for an explanation
> of this fine. If I don't get an answer, I shall start

> inquiries through the Italian consulate here. It would
> be better if you tell us.

Oh, brother. Why wouldn't they believe me?

The next day, this arrived:

> Your last letter didn't explain why you have to pay the
> police. Why do they want 10,000 lire from you every
> month? We checked with the Italian consulate, and
> they've never heard of such a thing. Are you in some
> kind of trouble? EXPLAIN.

On the third day, she called off the dogs:

> I received a letter from the Italian consulate here
> saying that they got my letter from the police of
> Perugia, and they said that no, you were not in trouble
> with the law, but the 10,000 lire must be for your
> tuition at school. You see, we paid a lump sum for
> your first three months last August, so now you will
> have to pay it each month, and we'll put the
> additional into your account. Do you understand?

Oh, yes, I understood. I understood that my parents went more ape shit over sending me an extra fifteen dollars per month than Grace drinking in cars with boys at three in the morning.

4

THE WARMTH OF STONE

For hundreds of years, Perugia's college students hung out on the tall steps of the San Lorenzo Cathedral in the main piazza, socializing, reading, or watching hill-town life.

One afternoon, after classes, I joined them on the warm marble steps to soak in the pale autumn sun. Looking around expectantly, I hoped to make new friends or admire the beautiful young Italian men.

"Where are you from?" asked one of three smiling Italian girls sitting nearby.

I leaned toward them, returning their smiles. "California."

Their eyebrows lifted in fascination. They had many questions, including, "Where in California?"

When I said, "Near San Francisco," one of the girls responded in English.

"Oh, Golden Gate Bridge."

Chiara, Stefania, and her sister, Lina, told me how they had grown up in Perugia. Ever patient, they tolerated my linguistic tangles before gently correcting me, sometimes with great charm and sometimes with laughter.

"Oh, can you translate a song for me?" asked Chiara. She pulled the English lyrics of a Pink Floyd song, "Money," from her backpack.

"I'll try." I wrote down a translation using my Italian dictionary and did lots of pantomiming before singing the song in my Italian lyrics, which was a trip.

"Oh," said Stefania, "when she sings in Italian, she has no accent."

Lina stood up and asked, "You want to get some gelato with us?"

We walked around a corner to a random gelateria, where I tasted the most intoxicating cinnamon-flavored gelato.

As we took our seats at an outdoor table, I felt lighter from a new sensation of freedom to do what I wanted when I wanted. I savored this delicious feeling after Mom's distrust. Now, instead of on repeat in my head, her nagging only existed in a letter I could put away.

Savoring the pleasure of my gelato, I felt my self-esteem skyrocket as I listened to Chiara, Stefania, and Lina chatter in my new language.

Chiara turned to me and said, "You should come with me to gather herbs in the countryside sometime."

"Oh," said Lina, "It's beautiful to be in the countryside."

I agreed that it sounded wonderful. As the autumn day grew chilly, the girls took me to another café, and we warmed up indoors by sipping hot milk and rum. Yum.

After a perfect afternoon with my new Italian girlfriends, we parted after we decided to take a day trip to Assisi the following Saturday.

"It'll be so fun!" said Lina.

I couldn't wait.

These friendships paid off in my Italian classes. One morning, when the professoressa called on me, I piped up with the correct answer.

I also saw how studying Italian would make me a better writer as I happily connected word meanings from English to Italian and back to Latin. If I ran into the English word "defenestrate," meaning to throw or jump from a window, I understood its meaning. The Italian word for window, "finestra," dovetails nicely into "defenestrate."

One day, our professoressa demonstrated my most important Italian lesson. "Even though it is proper to say it this way," she said, "it sounds too ugly." She wrinkled her nose and shook her head. "So, we say it improperly because it sounds more beautiful."

Then she smiled.

I sat back in my seat, my mind overflowing with astonishment. Making a language's beauty the highest concern? This made me adore Italian even more.

Alone in my room, I opened Mom's latest letter and found sweet notes from my three little brothers about how much they missed me. A sad smile crossed my face.

I had badly wanted to escape from home for my adventure abroad. And now I was paying the price of living so far from home—I'd never known loneliness until my whole world disappeared. I missed my family and our warm house always open, not just during our famous parties, to a constant parade of friends and relatives.

Tired of feeling sad, I unfolded Mom's letter and read her grumblings about the money I cost them and how I should appreciate this great opportunity.

But then her letter got confusing. After complaining about money, she wrote that I must visit our relatives all over Italy. And then she added, "Since it's the Catholic Church's Holy Year, you should make pilgrimages to all the basilicas."

How could I do this without spending more money?

I folded her letter, thinking there was no pleasing her. Yet I wanted to please her. So I decided to make her proud. I grabbed a pen and flimsy Italian air mail stationery to write her in Italian and express my gratitude.

My plan backfired when Dad wrote, "Don't write anymore in Italian. Your poor mother had to hunt down a translator. She found an Italian seamstress at the dry cleaners."

5

BEWARE OF DARKNESS

I spotted Gul during our morning break in the school's café while waiting with other girls for my cappuccino and croissant.

He was an older, beefy, Turkish man, and he walked over to bug me. Again. A tour guide from Istanbul, he always acted friendly, offering to buy my coffee. *Jesus.* For weeks I'd been telling him *no.* I even tried politely ignoring him.

But he never stopped.

And why go out with him when all I had to do was step outside to enjoy a veritable feast of gorgeous Italian guys my age? As a five-foot-two brunette with green eyes from my grandmother Grace DiPietro, I had pure Italian blood. I found better prospects than this creep around the piazza every day.

This time, he asked, "Come to dinner with me?"

And this November morning was different. He caught me in a moment of vulnerability. At the beginning of the month, with few lire in my wallet, I considered his offer of a free hot meal.

"But only at a restaurant in the piazza," I said. *Better for a clean getaway.*

When he agreed, his offer seemed safe.

I found Gul wearing an Italian overcoat in a growing dusk that evening. He stood with his roommate—a fellow Turkish tour guide—and an American girl I'd never met.

"We need to take a bus to the restaurant," said Gul, towering over me.

"But you said we're eating around here," I said, my voice tight.

I looked at the other American girl giggling with her date, and my wariness faded as we boarded a bus.

As we rode downhill into the suburbs, Gul said, "Now, we are going to our apartment to cook your dinner."

Fuck. My wariness roared back. I shot a glance at the other American girl, yet she showed no hint of fear.

Inside their second-floor apartment, we ate spaghetti and drank red wine around a small wooden table in a cramped kitchen, Gul constantly refilling my wine glass. I watched the American girl cuddle and coo with her date as I squirmed in my chair, antsy to leave.

I stood up when the other couple disappeared behind a door down a hallway. "Well, I should head back," I said, pulling on my sweater.

"Why don't you spend the night?" said Gul.

"No. No. Take me to the bus stop."

"But no buses run after ten o'clock."

My stomach hardened as anger raced through me. As I studied the deserted street through the kitchen window, helplessness crashed inside me.

Where was I? *Should I walk up the winding streets and search for the piazza? What if I get lost? Or get robbed or attacked?*

"I'll walk home," I said.

"Where will you go? You don't know much Italian."

Shit. "Can you call me a taxi?"

"No taxis here, either."

I remembered seeing a phone in the kitchen. I stepped away from the window and grabbed the heavy black receiver.

Dead. I slammed it down.

I was stuck.

Gul stood in the kitchen, smiling smarmily, and I hated him so much. With panic rising, I explored the apartment's hallway, Gul right behind me.

Fuck. There's got to be somewhere to sleep here, a sofa, something.

I found heavy French doors and threw them open into a living room. In the darkness, I made out stacked chairs, boxes, and tables on a hard terrazzo floor. Distressed, I walked faster down the hall, upset that Gul followed behind me.

"See? No place to sleep," he said.

My shaking hand twisted another doorknob. Great, a bathroom. And he was still behind me. Behind the last door in the hallway, I found a room with a narrow bed and a dirty Persian carpet—Gul's bedroom.

And he was still behind me when he shut the door.

I froze, wearing my dress and sweater, contemplating my situation. I couldn't sleep on the dirty Persian carpet, so I curled up into a fetal position atop the bed covers next to Gul, facing away from him, making it clear I was not interested in him.

Then I went numb.

My brain tried to shut down as his big leg forced my legs apart. As I fought him. As my hands pushed against his big bulky shoulders bearing down on me.

Then, everything else went blank.

Afterward, he slept like a baby.

All night long, I willed the early gray light to seep through the curtains. Though I lay motionless, he woke up and raped me again.

I've got to get out. I've got to get out.

As morning light bled into the room, I slipped from the bed and grabbed my leather boots. I couldn't move fast enough—the seconds passed like mud.

Silent, I stepped into the dark hallway, pulled on my boots, and left the apartment.

Outside, after escaping the crime scene, I released a breath of relief into the frigid air.

Free. Alone.

At the bus stop, I waited for a bus that didn't run that early.

Minutes passed before Gul walked up, asking, "Where'd you go?"

I ignored him and stepped away. We stood there for what seemed like a lifetime.

When the bus finally arrived, he climbed aboard behind me and sat next to me, scooting close, acting as if on a date. His bulk took up my seat, so I squished myself against the window, wrapped my sweater tightly around my waist, and stayed mute. Pressing my cheek against the hard glass, I stared outside as the bus heaved itself up the hill, curving toward the piazza.

After that wretched night, I flew into self-blame, believing I had lived too recklessly, believing the rape was my fault.

But having dinner at an apartment with two guys and another American woman wasn't reckless. No. I'd lost my innocence amid danger because a predator had found his prey.

Could I have saved myself?

Not when tricked, manipulated, and lied to. Not when overpowered. I couldn't fight off such a physically large man. Yet guilt consumed me since I believed I hadn't tried hard enough to make him stop.

He sat behind me in class, offering me coffee or dinner.

I irritably turned him down.

I ignored him.

I made him invisible.

I wrote in my journal, "I'm no longer a romantic." My words stung me like a bullet.

Violation, invasion, and abandonment threw me into isolation, and I began living as if nothing had happened.

I was only nineteen.

One dank morning, I awoke feeling an almost unbearable swirl of shock, disbelief, and powerlessness. To combat this feeling, I armored myself with long underwear and clothing layers, topped by my wool overcoat.

In survival mode, I checked my wallet to ensure I had enough money for protection. I also ensured I wouldn't be late for class since I had to learn Italian quickly and understand everything around me.

Outside, under an oppressive gray sky, I walked to school through Perugia's stony medieval heart, where no trees or landscaping adorned the narrow passages. A stink of dirty, musty, standing water hit my nose as I rounded a corner. I braced against the cold, ignoring the thousands of years of history layered beneath my feet. I climbed a marble staircase to class inside the palazzo, blind to its surrounding rococo riches.

Slow-walking into my classroom, I wrinkled my forehead with worry. What if Gul sat behind me again?

After checking out where my friends sat, I slipped into a lucky spot in front of an entire row of students. This stopped Gul from sitting behind me and asking me out.

Still, my nightmare came roaring back. I focused on my breathing to avoid full-blown panic.

During the morning break, I sat with South American girls in the school's café, chatting over cappuccinos and croissants.

"Mmmm. I'm reveling in the perfection of my pastry," I said.

I turned my head and caught Gul looking at me. Joy dissolved from my face as I crumbled inside.

That asshole.

I fled into the women's restroom and locked myself in a cubicle for solitude. Once my breath slowed, I stood up to flip open the lock. It didn't give. I jiggled it, tugged it, and kicked the door in frustration.

Not again! I'd had enough of these mysterious fucking Italian doors and locks. Furious, I crawled out from underneath the door or risked becoming the lock's prisoner for life.

I'd only been in Italy six weeks, and already, I had traveled a painful terrain. My life changed overnight; shock shut down my emotions, and I was consumed by helplessness, a feeling previously unfamiliar to me. He had overpowered me. I couldn't protect myself. I suffered, yet I didn't know how to stop it.

After Professoressa Franchini dismissed us, I fled my gilded classroom, its Venetian glass chandelier, ornate ceiling, and eighteenth-century desks, to fly away from my attacker. Alone, awash in humiliation, I couldn't say aloud what had happened. I fumbled through my days, convincing myself the attack wasn't a big deal, yet I drifted into a netherworld of amnesia and buried sorrow.

He sat in my class for the rest of the academic year, my back prickling whenever I felt his eyes on me.

6

UNCOMFORTABLY NUMB

I slammed my textbook shut and threw it onto my desk. Every night, I loathed being alone. I sat, contemplating how I couldn't write letters home though homesickness overwhelmed me. Sleep was impossible in my cold room, which my landlady lied about being heated at night.

I had to get out of there.

I grabbed my coat as restlessness drove me from my bare room into the night. In a fugue state, I walked uphill to Via Sant'Agata. After pressing a buzzer at a heavy wooden door, I retreated inside an upscale club's plush, red, womb-like interior, joining women in silk dresses and men in fine overcoats.

Back in Marin, I'd hated smoky bars and drank little, preferring to smoke weed before hiking on Mount Tamalpais with Jackson. Here in Italy, I fled into my new world every night, haunting this club among my new tribe.

"Hey, Lenore, what do you want to drink?" asked Adil, my Palestinian bartender. A black light bathed his long, curving white bar, and mirrors around the room reflected his white shirt in a purplish glow.

"I'll have a rum and cola."

Under a low vaulted ceiling, stone archways opened to a mirrored dance area. Sipping my drink, I wound through a crowd of students, businessmen, and foreigners.

I settled on a white leather banquette, illuminated by soft red lights and cigarettes glowing in the dark. After exchanging greetings, with kisses on both cheeks, I chatted with two girls from Milan reclining on their fur coats draped across the banquette. One offered me a Dunhill cigarette. Never a smoker, I had begun buying packs of Dunhills, which I could not afford. The red and gold packs felt reassuring, and the tobacco gave me a rush.

Sedated after my second drink, I watched two guys dance together in a mock tango. Across from me, men sat drinking, their bored faces glowing red from a globe on a low table. Their younger counterparts asked me to dance.

Tunes ran from fifties swing to British rock, American hits to ABBA and "Money" by Pink Floyd. Italians were nuts about Pink Floyd. The album, *The Dark Side of the Moon,* became the soundtrack of my Italian year.

Drinking and smoking, I laughed at terrible Italian jokes, learned how to swing dance, and socialized until the wee hours. Then I stumbled home through the damp streets, drunk, deadened, and careless about my safety, serenaded by the lone whine of a Fiat slipping into low gear. I hoped clubbing would help numb me and assuage my pain—or distract me from it.

But drinking and smoking too much and not sleeping enough wasn't healthy. I knew this. This wasn't me. I had never gone to bars alone at home. But now, in Italy, I couldn't stop myself, hating to stay home alone and lie in bed with my dark thoughts.

My teenage mind thought, *Why not go out, laugh, and dance until exhausted?*

In the morning, on my way to class, my eyes burned from cigarette smoke. My hangover headache worsened as cars beeped, church bells pealed, and colorfully dressed schoolchildren chattered with their chic mothers. I trudged to school, surrounded by vibrant Italian life, and felt like the only frozen person in the world.

One night, fighting loneliness in my room, I rolled over on my bed and pushed my homework aside. I couldn't concentrate. What was happening to me?

Staring at the ceiling, I remembered how I hadn't fought Gul. I'd known he could overpower me, so I froze.

I said *no* many times, didn't I? But he never stopped. I shut out what was happening and disassociated myself from my body.

If someone told me, "Lenore, it was rape," I would've argued how it was all my fault. I drank wine at dinner. I went into the bedroom. I must've sent out messages that I wanted sex.

I'd had so much to look forward to this year, and now I was dealing with *this*. With no one to shield or soothe me, I wondered where it had all unraveled—when I had failed to learn about protecting myself. My mind wandered back to high school, during my junior year, when I was sixteen.

My Catholic high school didn't offer sex education, only a disappointing Love and Marriage class; girls and boys were taught in separate classes. We didn't learn anything about what the public school kids talked about, such as sexually transmitted diseases or birth control. The only birth control I had learned about was the rhythm method after Mom accidentally got pregnant with twins Angelo and Ricci when I was ten.

Instead, our teachers taught us useless information:

1. Your body is a temple of the Holy Ghost.
2. Don't have sex.
3. Have sex after you get married.

One day after class, I told my best friend Jenny, "We're not learning what the public school kids are learning, like stuff about sex diseases or birth control. I only know about that useless rhythm method!"

Jenny laughed.

Much later, she confided that she had gotten pregnant at fifteen and hid her abortion from me for a year.

Wow. She was a perfect example of how keeping innocent young girls ignorant could spectacularly backfire.

"Why didn't you tell me?" I asked.

"I just . . . it's too embarrassing."

"I'm so sorry," I said.

"It was horrible, Lenore. When I was waking up, I heard the nurses say, 'She's so young. She's just a baby herself.'"

"Oh, Jenny, how awful."

It was time for us to go to class, so we separated, and I burned inside. Why couldn't we have real sex education like the public school kids? It was so frustrating.

Yet, as teenagers who thought we knew it all, Jenny and I had carried on as if nothing had changed and everything was normal. But without a true sex education, we remained ignorant, dangerously so.

Forced to pay a high price for our school's foolhardy "sex education," Jenny learned her consequences the hard way and lived with a shame that never should've belonged to her.

And what about me? I used to believe women only got raped in dark alleys and by strange men. Now, in the cruelest way, I had learned that wasn't true.

If I had been taught how to protect myself, I could've avoided the worst trauma of my life. It terrified me that the very adults who guided and protected me had chosen to keep me ignorant and defenseless against dangers they refused to name.

One day before afternoon class, my diminutive yet commanding landlady stopped me in her foyer.

"I never see you study, and you always come home late at night," she said.

I stared at her face, carefully decoding her Italian. What the hell was this all about?

"Are you a student at the university?"

"Yes, I am," I answered, in halting Italian.

"Show me your student ID."

"Of course." I dug into my backpack and displayed my registration card. She gave it a cursory glance.

"Also, Signora, when will you turn on the heat at night? I'm starting to get a bad cough."

"Soon, soon," she said. But her eyes said she was lying to me.

After a cough erupted to punctuate my point, I said. "Please, I ask many times. I pay extra for my heating oil."

"Yes, yes," she said, walking away.

Leaving the building, I wondered what was so bad about going out every night and enjoying my new life. *Jesus.* I came home every afternoon for a nap, just like the Italians did.

Was it because high-spirited American girls lived freely and independently, accountable to no one? Was that why she treated me as if I were shady?

I decided to find a new pension with more heat and less scowling disapproval.

One morning in early November, my chest rumbled with the gravel of my coughs. I rubbed my face, tired from a rough night. Unable to escape the memory of my hands pushing against Gul's bulky shoulders, I jumped out of bed and distracted myself by splashing cold water on my face.

I saw outside my window how winter had blown in overnight, blanketing Perugia's stone center with snow. As I bundled up for school, I wrapped my muffler around my neck and donned a knit hat and gloves, never needed in Mill Valley, to muddle through another day.

Fortunately, before class began, I found a seat far from Gul. Still, just the sight of him caused me to ruminate about what he did, distracting me from the professoressa's lecture.

He deserved to get arrested and punished. But if I told the police, they'd blame me, the American girl. I could hear their questions already: *Are you a virgin? Why did you go to a man's apartment unless you wanted sex? Why lie, Signorina?*

No, there would be no justice for me.

Since I didn't attend through a US university program, I lacked student support, and my school lacked counselors.

Worse, my father couldn't protect me; he always went after anyone who hurt me, but now, my warrior chieftain was an ocean away.

In eighth grade, classmate bullies had tricked me into searching for a non-existent basketball game at an empty public high school at night.

Through my devastation and tears, I told my parents how they laughed at my stupidity for falling for their prank. The following day, Dad headed straight to Reverend Mother's office.

Then, Reverend Mother surprised my class by ordering, "All those involved, come into the hallway. Cameron, Scott, Alex, and Marcy."

Afterward, I told Dad how she had slapped them with suspensions.

He said, "She better! I asked her, 'What the hell, Reverend Mother? Who are you educating here? A bunch of Hells Angels? My daughter was alone, wandering the high school alone at night! That wasn't safe!'"

Recalling this memory, I ached for Dad's comfort and protection here in Italy. We'd go to the police together because they'd believe a father and a man. But I could never tell Dad what had happened. I was too ashamed.

A cold realization sank in. I was on my own for the first time in my life.

"Correct, Lenore?" asked my professoressa.

My attention snapped back to the classroom.

"I will repeat. In this case, is that the correct past-tense form?"

I stammered my wrong answer. The professoressa sniffed, not at all pleased with me.

Each day, I walked home after class, straightening my spine, staying stoic, getting by on wits alone. I tried my best to put that night behind me, hiding my pain well. Some memories wouldn't fade. Around town, reminders waited. The shape of a man's overcoat on the street. The silhouette of a bus stop at night. Though much of that night was clouded in amnesia, the parts I did remember clung to me, refusing to dissolve.

I was no longer the girl who had arrived here, wide-eyed and ready for adventure. I had transformed into a ghost of a girl, silently changing into a freaked-out, depressed young woman.

By day, I told myself this was the most beautiful time of my life. I wrote about how much I loved Italy and scrawled the words into my journal, urging myself to *savor it*—the foreign streets, the adventure—I knew wouldn't last forever.

But by night, I found it hard to go home. My room felt suffocating, too quiet, too still. In the unbearable silence, the truth pressed in, undeniable. I tried focusing on my studies, but my thoughts jumbled. I'd stare at my notebook, the words swimming, my mind slipping. Eventually, I abandoned my struggle and grabbed my coat, surrendering to the restlessness pulling me back into the night. It was the only way I could bury that ghost within me.

I'd order my anesthetic drink, downing one after another until the dance floor spun. In the morning, I'd wake up and start the cycle over again—drink, dance, collapse into bed, wake up, pretend.

Deep down, I knew the truth. I couldn't outrun what was already inside me.

Desperate to sleep somewhere warm at night as my coughs worsened, I found a temporary place to stay, a dormitory run by nuns and recommended by the school housing office. My Italian girlfriends Stefania, Chiara, and Lina accompanied me to check it out.

A gentle nun told me, "Yes, you can stay here until you find a permanent home. We offer hot water daily and heat all night."

Surprised by her generosity, I made her repeat her words in two languages to ensure I understood her correctly.

"Wonderful, thank you!" I said, almost kissing her.

Two hours later, I said, "Arrivederci" to my fascist landlady and moved in with the nuns.

7

TRANSLATING RESPECT

Heavy, fortified doors separated the men's and women's areas. The nuns ensured that men and women barely mixed, but there was a common room where everyone was allowed to mingle. This is where I met David.

"Please, Signorina?" His open, round face towered over me.

I looked up at his ebony face. How odd it felt to smile that evening, feeling so alone in Italy.

In clipped, halting Italian, David asked me to translate an American song for him and his fellow Nigerian students—the group, expectant and sincere, watched from across the dayroom.

"Okay, which one?" I asked.

David turned up the volume on his battered cassette player, and I took in the unmistakable earthy notes of Aretha Franklin's timeless song, "Respect."

I couldn't help but smile and nod. "Of course."

Oozing sexuality, Aretha belted out her hit, and I grappled with translating a sexual, molten African American soul song in a windowless common room in a nuns' dormitory. To Nigerians.

"Well, she has what you want . . ."

"Yes?"

"But all she needs is your respect, you know, *rispetto.*"

To me, the Italian word rispetto sounded too chaste. Respect involves much more than taking a new lover like Aretha meant.

As she settled the respect question to clear the way for other business, a chilling realization struck me, and that night came rushing back. Gul believed he'd found a girl so innocent, so unaware, that she wouldn't demand respect. But he was wrong.

I deserved to be heard. I deserved to leave when I wanted. A single "no" should have been enough to stop him if he had respected me. The injustice of his violation pulsed through my heart, blood, and bones. Too naïve, too scared, I hadn't even thought to demand what I deserved.

Hell, I shouldn't have had to demand it at all. And that broke my heart. I had come to Italy for a year to become a writer. Instead, that year was becoming about survival.

Back to the task at hand, as I scribbled each heated lyric in English for David, our dictionaries came out: English and Italian, Italian and Nigerian.

Smiling, I got into the music, singing along with Aretha as the Nigerians grinned and laughed, crowding their knees toward me as we sat on the hard furniture. I sat back, relaxed—feeling comfortable and safe around men—for the first time in months.

Aretha continued to drive her point home as her backup singers chanted behind her. Yet I failed to conquer the Italian-English-Nigerian divide; my Italian words came off as too dainty.

"Ah . . . un po' di più?" I said, frustrated. "A little more? No, that's not right. A little bit."

Asking for respect just a little bit will not fly. I will demand it, no matter what, from men, from the police if I tell them, from the entire culture here.

I pressed on. The clock on the wall revealed our curfew was fast approaching, and Aretha swooned about her lover's kisses as sweet as honey, but, hey, so was her money.

At this, the Nigerians roared and slapped each other, bending over with laughter. Oh, yeah, Aretha was sassy.

Finally, my Waterloo: that sixties catchphrase, "Sock it to me."

"Like hit? She wants to be hit?" asked David.

"No, no, American . . ." I raced through my dictionary for the right word. "Slang."

Now, their long fingers spun the pages of the Nigerian dictionary.

"It's like, it's like she wants him to love her right now," I said, avoiding the temptation to do any pantomiming.

Trading glances, their expressions slowly changed, some with sly grins as others averted their eyes with embarrassment.

"American slang," said David. "Okay."

Amid dictionaries, hand gestures, and my translation among my new friends, we all laughed. My sad reality faded, and I felt pure joy, so different after living with the fear and loneliness I experienced because of Gul. In those moments of friendship, song, and healing laughter, I saw how much I needed all of it.

As the minutes ticked away, David rewound the tape; we all stood up and sang the entire song together, shouting out each letter of the word "respect."

When our curfew arrived, we sang at the top of our voices in camaraderie. I reveled in Aretha showing me the power and strength to demand respect and accept nothing less.

As the song concluded for the final time, as her last healing words washed over me, I experienced a crack of light after many dark moments, and I promised myself, "I will make Aretha's song my own."

8

BESIEGED

At the nuns' dorm, I slept on a bunk bed among many others in a long room. I quickly became unpopular with my female roommates who couldn't sleep because of my constant hacking all night from bronchitis.

One morning, a girl commanded, "Bloody hell! Go see a doctor!"

No worries. After I find my new place, that's next on my list.

That afternoon, my Italian girlfriends and I checked out a comfortable pension room in a hip, boho quarter where students found cheap rooms near the PostModernissimo movie house.

As the landlady stood by, Chiara opened and inspected the armoire, and Lina tested the bed. Stefania opened the green wooden window shutters and said, "You have a clothesline for laundry out here."

I crossed the hall to investigate a large bathroom and turned on the tap. I almost yelped with joy.

"Yes, it's hot water day," said the landlady. After my Italian girlfriends translated the rental terms, I paid the first month's rent—equivalent to forty

US dollars a month, heating oil extra—at Via Cartolari, 22.

After a glorious hot bath that evening, I wrote a letter home from my new address, armoring myself against an onslaught of questions about my move. At least I'd enjoy three weeks of peace as our letters made their tortuous journey through Italy's postal service.

I unpacked a plastic bag stuffed with my letters from home and snuggled into my bed to re-read them. I laughed again at Grace's written warning: "By the way, Mom reads ALL the letters you send me. In fact, she opens them before I get home, so be careful! She says, 'I told Lenore I would read all her letters.' Nosy Norma."

I also re-opened one of Jackson's letters, his reply to my letter about the night I had been raped. And how awful it was.

"Jeez, I'm sorry to hear about that creep," he had written from far away California. "I cringed while reading it. I mean, every time I go to another country, it even happens to me. So please watch out."

I knew about Jackson's near misses with sexual assault, propositions, and groping, once by a Moroccan in Paris and again by a hostel keeper in Mexico.

Had he avoided disaster as a man who said no? As a man who demanded respect? Upon re-reading his letter, I thought I'd see more alarm from him.

But no one understood how my attack colored every part of my life now, from how I dressed every morning to how I dreaded walking alone at night from the club unless I was hammered.

I slumped with shame. How could I have let this happen? Why didn't I follow my instincts and leave? But where? How?

I couldn't tell anyone what happened, couldn't make the words leave my mouth. And I could *never* tell my parents. They'd freak out and blame me, yell at me, and order me home while branding me promiscuous. They wouldn't give me the respect I deserved either. They'd only see me as their irresponsible daughter who couldn't be trusted out in the world.

Surviving alone, I stared at the ground as I walked from school, struggling in the frigid winter in my red leather boots with a broken heel on the cobblestones of an Italian hill town.

Back in my room, I scribbled in my journal, my head full of novels, short stories, paintings, and pictures; so many ideas exploded inside my head with nowhere to land except on those pages.

But my heart sank as I re-read what I had written over the last three months, seeing a besieged girl within those scrawled pages. Had I forever lost my old, sunny self?

Sheltered by family and church as a Catholic schoolgirl in the second grade.
Image courtesy of the author's collection.

I stared at my desk, listing everything I saw: a candle, textbooks, a coffee cup, a perfume bottle, an Italian-English dictionary, letters from home, tattered copies of the *Daily American* newspaper, a lipstick tube, an empty mineral water bottle, a stack of 3,000 lire, my school notebook.

I stared at my insurmountable assignments, head in my hands. Accustomed to pulling high marks during my first two years at the College of Marin, I thought I'd studied hard enough, but despite my quick affinity for Italian, my mind got stuck. Unable to muster the energy to form thoughts, my grades fell off, casualties of my trauma.

One night, I dreamed of being back in Mill Valley as a little girl in my green plaid uniform, dancing from foot to foot, waiting outside Our Lady of Mount Carmel School for Mom to pick me up. I happily slid into our familiar station wagon.

"Let's go home," Mom said. As she drove, I relaxed in the back seat, feeling warmth, unconditional love, and complete safety.

Cruelly, I awoke in a dim, cold room. I pulled myself out of bed to fire up my oil heater and crawled back under the covers. I picked up my journal while waiting for my room to warm up. As I paged through it, a coldness stuck inside me. I had left home for freedom as a young artist, alive in Italy, with my whole life before me. Then, sexual violence turned everything sideways. I'd gotten a lethal dose of reality, a drug too strong, too heavy to handle, so I'd picked up my crown of thorns, woven of blame and humiliation, and placed it atop my head.

Tears filled my eyes, recalling how much hope I'd had about my year in Perugia. Now, I lived unprotected, far from home and family, and weary from the raw ache of homesickness living in my gut.

As I read more entries, a sudden electrical shock ran through me. I'd written no entries between November 7th and December 1st. A stolen month. More proof that, after Gul forced himself on me, I was frozen. Traumatized. A ghost.

9

LIKE A LAMB
TO SLAUGHTER

One night at the club, the DJ turned up Tina Turner's growl on her latest hit, "Nutbush City Limits," an ode to her simple Tennessee hometown. A sudden thrust of homesickness stabbed me.

I thought about my dad and how much I missed him. There was so much I hadn't known before leaving home, and now Dad was too far away to help me. Isolation and helplessness soaked through me with a shudder.

Sex had morphed for me into a weapon, the source of my secret woundedness. Instead of an expression of passion like I'd shared with Jackson, sex now was nothing more than a harrowing brutality.

Growing up, my curiosity and longing to understand the mystery of sex were blocked. In the eighth grade, as my thirteen-year-old body transformed, the nuns showed us girls a film about puberty; the boys had their own to watch.

During question time, crushed with frustration, I had many questions, but not for nuns. And not with boys around. In exasperation, I listened to a nun explain conception as a miracle that happens after a man and woman pray for a child.

This drove me to Mom as my only hope for answers. So, after school, as she cooked dinner, I said, "So, how do the egg and sperm get together?"

She looked like she had just choked on something, but then she placed a lid on her boiling pasta pot and ushered me into her bedroom.

"You'll find out on your wedding night."

My mouth dropped open. "What? I gotta wait that long?"

"Well, *I* had to."

God, when it comes to sex, things sure get strange. I guessed I'd have to figure things out for myself.

And things only got stranger, especially after Dad drove us through Haight-Ashbury one Sunday and bought a hippie newspaper, *The Oracle*, from a street hawker. I opened it to a full page displaying psychedelic artwork of a naked couple in a Kama Sutra position.

Intrigued, I viewed the page from all angles, trying to learn something.

"Gimme that!" Dad reached over the back seat and snatched the paper from my hands.

On another night, Dad came home from work, furious. "God damn it," he fumed to Mom in the kitchen. "I drove through Sausalito, and two hippies were doing it like dogs in the park!"

Confused about his anger, I asked, "What happened?"

Mom said, "Never mind."

My parents' silence around sex maddened me, so I headed to Mill Valley's library with my unanswered questions and solved them by devouring books. Once I learned the full details, I thought, *Well, this all seems pretty simple. What's all the mystery about?*

One night, Mom invaded the Patchouli-scented bedroom I shared with Grace as we sat on our beds doing homework. She drew our drapes against the night outside and sat next to me.

"My God, Lenore, I knew that smell was coming from here," she said, waving her hand before her nose. "You smell like an Algerian whorehouse!"

"How do you know what an Algerian whorehouse smells like, Mom?"

"You're only thirteen. That hippie perfume is much too strong for a young girl. Give it to me."

"It's all used up." I lied. I closed my binder and tossed my pencil onto our nightstand. "Mom, remember how you said I could date when I was sixteen?"

Grace's eyes shot up from her schoolbook.

Mom pursed her lips, not thrilled about my question. "Well, you're thirteen now so, I don't know. Maybe when you're sixteen, but if you do, we'd have to meet him first."

"Okay," I said. *Three years is a long time.*

"But don't let him get too touchy," she said, frowning. "No hands down your blouse or anything like that."

"Okay," I said, frustrated. Then, I tried to pin her down, which she hated. "So that's it? I can date when I'm sixteen?"

"Don't get smart, young lady."

And there it was, another non-answer from Mom. Then, she left our bedroom because the twins had started fighting in the living room.

All I wanted was a cute, sexy boyfriend. And all she wanted was to tell me how boys would make me do things I didn't want to do.

What were Mom and Dad so frightened about? If they worried I'd get pregnant, wouldn't they want me to have sex education?

Over the years, restless feelings and curiosity blossomed inside me with nowhere to go. I had questions for Mom, yet she always provided vague, meaningless answers.

I had to skate through adolescence, lacking the knowledge or tools to develop a healthy sexuality or to understand the dangers of the darker side of sex.

By forcing me to stay naïve and innocent, my parents, the nuns, priests, and lay teachers—hell, even the Catholic Church—had sent me into the world like a lamb to slaughter.

10

TINA TURNER BURNS IT DOWN

One Sunday during my sixteenth summer, as Dad's opera records filled the air, he asked, "Hey, Lenore, want to go see the Ike and Tina Turner Revue?"

It was so weird that Dad wanted to take Grace and me to see them because he was a Republican—and Ike and Tina weren't tame.

"Do I! God, that would be so far out," I answered.

I'd seen psychedelic posters advertising their past shows at the Fillmore Auditorium, but surely Dad wasn't taking us to the ground zero of San Francisco counterculture. Other times he'd crossed the bridge into the City, he'd taken Mom to the Fairmont Hotel to hear Lena Horne. Or he took us all to the Broadway musical *Oliver*. But never to an actual *concert*. And once, on a school night, he took me to *Madame Butterfly* at the San Francisco Opera. *Boring opera*.

As I sat with all those rich people, I still felt a bit stoned from an after-school joint. But when Puccini's tragedy ended, and Dad stood to leave, I stayed stuck in my seat, blinking back tears, speechless and heartbroken.

And now, I was going to see Tina Turner, live, in concert!

"But aren't they playing at the Fillmore?" I said.

"They're playing at the Circle Star Theatre. In the Peninsula," he said. That made more sense. "So, *you* like Tina?"

"She's great," said Dad, a former band musician. "What a performer! I bet she puts on a great show."

During that summer, Ike and Tina's cover was playing all over the airwaves. I loved it. And before the Ike and Tina Turner Revue hit town this time, I chronicled my excitement in my journal, writing, "Wow! I can't wait! I can't wait to feel their power and excitement. It's going to be a blast."

The days crawled by, until, on a Friday afternoon, I threw open my closet doors, excitedly searching for something to wear to the concert.

We took our seats in a crowd of black people and white people, old people like my parents, and kids like my sister and me.

As soon as I sat, I began twisting my hands. I thought about the time my friends and I saw the Rolling Stones concert movie *Gimme Shelter* and Ike and Tina performed this one dirty song, "I've Been Loving You Too Long."

And I hoped they wouldn't play it tonight. That would be such a bummer with all that blow-job business. I'd just die. After all, my parents didn't know how much I knew about sex from library books and reading *Ms.* magazine and *Rolling Stone.* And from hearing about what other girls did with their boyfriends. But I didn't know everything.

The pounding beats vibrated through me like a jet engine when the band began blasting on stage. A line of three Ikettes shimmied out in silver microminis. Then, Tina burst onstage like a hurricane, so sexy and dancing like a female Mick Jagger. She whirled around in a minidress dripping with rhinestone fringe that swung across her thighs. In high heels, she matched every beat of the music with precision and grace, gliding across the stage with fast, sharp footwork, ending in high-energy kicks. Intensely charismatic, she built a fierce connection with her audience with her raw sensuality and stunning vocal power.

Her stage presence amazed me; she seemed so free, sliding along, singing, and moving her hips like that. Her energy lifted me and made me feel like anything was possible.

Tina worked so hard on that stage that her skin glistened with sweat as she sang "River Deep—Mountain High" and "I Want to Take You Higher." She sustained her explosive energy throughout every song, and when she finished, we shouted for more.

The stage suddenly went silent. She grabbed her mic and began to sing "Proud Mary." She started with a slow, rolling tempo, then built up to a loud and fast crescendo. I jumped and howled with the rest of the crowd. Our roars felt like thunder, and I wondered if the roof would burst open.

I looked at my parents. They had also leaped from their seats, Dad wearing a huge smile.

Everything about this night was perfect.

But then, there it was. That song. The opening notes of "I've Been Loving You Too Long" streamed from Tina's mouth, amplified at a terrifyingly loud volume. And disaster collided into my excitement.

Oh, shit! Please, God, no! The lyrics were even dirtier than I'd remembered.

I sank into my seat and froze as Tina begged Ike to give it to her, *over and over,* what she needed and wanted. She writhed and groaned, caressing the phallic microphone as Ike made slurping, sucking noises. Forcing myself not to look at my parents, I cringed. If only I could've disappeared.

The song seemed to go on and on as if it were never going to end.

I waited forever for its crashing climax, which the crowd loved. Tina stood fearless and proud, her white smile blazing. She wasn't embarrassed at all, not like me.

Something shifted for me in that moment. Upfront on the stage, Tina showed me that the subject of sex could be really fun and exciting. And without guilt. She held nothing back as I cowered next to my parents, who didn't want me to have sex until I was old and married.

I prayed nobody would talk about that song during the long ride home. So I filled the silent car with, "That was so far out, wow! Thanks, Dad. I really enjoyed it. I love Tina."

"So did I," said my sister.

Mom turned to Dad and said, "Oh, Len, that was too much. I'm sure that goes over well in Vegas, but these girls didn't need to see that kind of stuff."

Oh, but I *did* need to see that kind of stuff. That was reality. I was too used to my parents keeping secrets about how the real world worked. Now that more truth had been unleashed, I was paying attention, and there was no going back.

11

MY PHYSICIAN MISSION

I awoke with a jerk, suffocating. *Oh, shit, not again.* Coughing and gasping for air, I sat up in a predawn darkness. My worsening cough threw me into abrupt fits day and night in Umbria's moist winter air. As I stuffed down my anguish to function, my lungs couldn't stop forcing it out.

After the sun came up, I crawled out of bed and staggered to the public telephone office to call home.

"Mom, I need money for a doctor," I rasped during our transatlantic call. "I can't stop coughing."

"Are you okay?" she asked.

I unconsciously lapsed into Italian. "No, mi sento malissimo—I mean, I feel awful."

She agreed to send the cash. Inside the phone booth, my legs weakened beneath me, and I said, "I've got to go, Mom."

Dizzy and worn out, I hung up.

When my money arrived, I consulted with my Italian girlfriends, Stefania, Chiara, and Lina.

"Go to the medical school's health clinic," they told me.

After diagnosing chronic bronchitis, the doctor prescribed an antibiotic. The pharmacist then handed me a strange pile of small powder packets and a package of feather-light, papery wafers—the exact wafers used as Communion hosts during Catholic Mass.

Too sick to make sense of this, I followed the pharmacist's instructions. Three times a day, I placed a wafer on my palm, moistened it with water, and emptied a powder packet. I pinched everything together like a fortune cookie and swallowed it.

The next day, Mom's express letter arrived.

> I hope by now you have seen a doctor. Find out with X-rays if you have TB. You could pick up strange bugs and fungi, too—especially in Perugia where there are students from all over the world. You don't want to end up with pneumonia. You've had this cough since November.
>
> Don't get drunk so much. Have you a problem? (Alcohol is a drug!)

That letter proved why I never confided in Mom about my struggles. Too harsh and too demanding, she always ensured I was in the wrong.

Attempting to survive physically and emotionally in hostile territory, I refused to voice the truth about my life in Italy. I still believed my parents wouldn't have believed me anyway. And instead of understanding that I was a victim of a serious crime, they'd probably tell me that they wouldn't support my promiscuity. I was too immature, they'd say, to traipse off alone to Europe and force me to return home right away. No, I'd never have risked it. I could've never gone home.

Though my life was almost too much to endure, I also loved living in Italy. I just wished Mom could've found a drop of compassion for me or showed some empathy as I battled illness and loneliness.

Swept away by exhaustion, I rolled another Communion wafer with the powder, swallowed it, and crashed into bed.

12

OF STONE

Living under fire and battling to get better, I felt fortunate that some illuminating moments made it easier to stick it out and finish my school year.

One important moment arrived in an envelope sent by my Aunt Eleanor in Ohio. It was the most important letter I'd received in Italy—from my grandfather, Arcangelo. I had written him in Italian from his homeland; my aunt said he kept my two letters in his wallet, making them available to show everyone.

"He was so proud and remarked how nice you wrote in Italian," she wrote. "You made him very happy with your little personal letters."

With trembling fingers, I unfolded his note and slowly translated his round hand into English:

Columbus, Ohio

Dearest granddaughter Lenora [sic] Asiano,
    Finally responding to your two letters, please
excuse my delay in which you brought me splendid

and good news about our relatives and the land where I was born. With any opportunity now that my family grew up in America, rich in opportunity, I don't tell you other than to give many greetings to my sisters and all my nephews. I'm sorry that I couldn't know them personally. Now I won't tell you anything other than I greet you with great love and conduct your studies—remain in memory:

—Honor

—Science

—And Health

is what nobody must ever forget.

Always your grand Papa,

Arcangelo DiPietro

Excuse my mistakes. I am ninety-three years old.

Born in 1882, he left Italy at twenty-one in 1903 and arrived in America with nothing but a pocket full of hope. Months later, after he earned her passage, the pregnant Graziella (Grace), his fifteen-year-old bride, followed him into the unknown. They hailed from hardscrabble Introdacqua and Sulmona, villages in Abruzzo's craggy mountains. Both uneducated, Arcangelo and Grace found the guts to cross an ocean to an unknown future in a strange country with an unfamiliar language, leaving behind family roots tracing back to the early 1700s.

After settling in Columbus, Ohio, by the twenties, they planted the seedlings of a substantial extended family in a two-story brick building housing their Italian mom-and-pop corner grocery and a large home with extra bedrooms for boarders.

A stonemason by trade, Arcangelo constructed stone walls on the boundary of his large lot. He thriftily gathered Ohio River Valley limestone and bordered a backyard where his tomatoes thrived, and my grandmother tended her beloved roses.

I always believed that he built his stone walls to create a bit of Italy on his plot in his new land. Did his walls symbolize his American dream, the dream that led him away from poverty?

As I held his short, innocent letter, tears welled in my eyes. I felt his regret over leaving his sisters behind and never knowing his nephews as his American family bloomed. His gift, this moment of grace, warmed my heart.

His letter made me think about my ancestors' history and fortitude. My grandfather's surname was DiPietro, which means "of stone." He was a humble stonemason who built the stone foundation upon which my family stood.

And I now stood on their shoulders. I had their blood in my veins, and this meant I was made of strong stuff, too.

Another tender moment clarified how staying in Italy was the right decision. Late one Saturday night in Caffè Turreno, I ran into Paolo, who ran in my Italian girlfriends' crowd. An art student at the Italian university and always up for adventure, he once had taken me on a motorcycle tour outside of town, past farmer fields and filthy gypsy camps.

His green eyes sparked as he enticed me to "come and see something marvelous."

I felt my curiosity building inside, so I joined him.

Walking after midnight, Paolo led me through quiet streets, damp stones glistening beneath our feet. A pale, discreet glow from the windows above cast an ethereal light, creating a mysterious atmosphere. When Paolo turned into a narrow, pitch-black alley, I realized I had no idea where he was taking me.

Impulsively, my stomach twisted as fear overtook me, and racing thoughts swirled in my head. *Oh, no. What's happening? I should turn around. I can't be here. It's not safe.*

But I didn't stop. I only said, "Paolo, where are we going?" as he continued leading me to an unknown, cavernous place.

"Here." He gestured extravagantly with his hand and opened a heavy wooden door.

A stocky man dusted in flour from head to toe, wearing a white apron and a round cap, welcomed us inside with a hearty, "Come in."

My trepidation dissipated.

Paolo and I followed the man into a dim, vaulted space enveloped in intense heat and humidity. I quickly pulled off my coat, hat, and muffler. We had entered a forno, or bakery, as the baker shuffled in felt slippers around a tall industrial scale. My eyes widened with awe and wonder; an intoxicating scent of baked goods, comforting and nostalgic, hit my nostrils.

In this steamy, surreal scene, ancient brick ovens lined the wall, and tall cooling racks groaned under the weight of pizzas and pastries. Beyond an archway stood trays of pastry shipments of all sizes and shapes. At long tables, bakers worked in swirling clouds of flour; their rhythmic kneading, mixing, and pounding transported me to another world. Others tossed handfuls of chopped garlic, onions, salt, and olive oil onto dough circles on long-handled wood paddles.

When they nodded hello to Paolo, I recognized his innate connection to this place. Knowing he wanted to share this special place with me, I felt a warmth spread throughout my chest.

"Today is pizza day," said our host.

"God, it smells delicious here," I said, almost light-headed from the aromas.

Hearing my accent, he asked, "Where are you from?"

"She's a student from California attending the foreigners' school," said Paolo.

"California? That's so far away."

A familiar pang of homesickness tugged my heart. Yes, in this underground scene, I was very far from home.

"How do you know him?" I asked Paolo.

He looked at me. "I grew up here. I know everyone! Hey, are you hungry? Want something to eat?"

Paolo gestured to a small table with two chairs. When we sat down, a tray of fresh, fragrant croissants landed on our table.

"Oh, my God." A sense of gratitude and contentment welled inside me. I'd been so hungry lately.

Stuffing a pastry into his mouth, Paolo grinned and mumbled, "Good, huh?"

I bit into my feathery croissant. "Wonderous."

We chatted as an aromatic pizza arrived. As we ate, I studied Paolo's handsome face framed by his sandy hair. He had always been sweet to me, but now, I saw him as unique. As sugary smells wafted in the air, I now understood how he saw me. To Paolo, I wasn't another American girl on the loose and in danger. I was a girl who'd come to an unfamiliar place to open her eyes to beauty, wonder, and delicious food.

I smiled, and then, feeling shy about being caught in a vulnerable moment, I looked around the bakery. "How old is this place?"

"Maybe hundreds of years old."

We chatted away as more decadence arrived: rocciata—a puff pastry stuffed with walnuts, sugar, and apples—and my favorite, a custard-filled confection called pasticciotto. Closing my eyes, I savored each mouthful— a million times better than hitting Jack in the Box in the wee hours back in Mill Valley. *Ah, the simple joys of Italian life.*

Later, I followed Paolo blissfully outside, content that I had trusted him as he led me into a black passageway late at night. I wouldn't have discovered that serendipitous pastry paradise if I hadn't. These adventures made staying in Italy worthwhile. Maybe I didn't need to feel afraid all the time, and that idea filled me with the hope that my inner pain might fall away. Not everything in Italy had to be tainted by one traumatic night.

Paolo left me with his usual goodbye as we headed home in different directions.

"Be careful!" he called out.

And I felt safe for the first time in weeks.

13

OPEN SEASON ON AMERICAN GIRLS

Just before Lent in February, Carnevale arrived. On the Saturday night before Ash Wednesday, I stood before the mirror on my armoire, fashioning a costume. I donned a long gypsy skirt, draped myself with scarves, and painted my face like a mime. A long night of parties lay ahead of me.

I weaved through crowds toward my first Carnevale bash of the night. Inside a packed student apartment, partiers wearing masks and costumes mingled as Grateful Dead music played. I accepted a glass of wine, but when someone fired up a spliff, I freaked out. Stories had swirled among students about arrests for simply smoking marijuana or how Nigerians convicted of dealing weed got life sentences. The second I smelled dope, I shot out the door in terror of landing in an Italian prison.

I wasn't in libertine Marin County anymore.

I pushed my way through packed streets to my next party, a blast thrown by my American buddies Danny and Art. They attended medical school at the Italian university, taking courses conducted in Italian, an impressive feat. I wondered how they found the time to throw their frequent ribald parties.

Entering their tiny apartment, I crammed into a loud mob of Italian and international students, now disguised as gypsies, nurses, nuns, priests, and the Pope himself. I searched for my hosts and found a bloodied Danny bandaged like a mummy and attached to an IV as Art pushed his immobile patient about in a wheelbarrow.

Music boomed, and people began to dance. I drew deeper into the chaos and bumped into a "peasant" wearing a black beret and holding a basket with country wine and a live rabbit. Someone shoved a bottle of wine into my hands, and I took a guzzle.

"Hey, Lenore," yelled Eddie from New York over the music. "I was talking to someone about you when I was in Morocco."

"Huh? I don't know anyone in Morocco."

I spotted Paolo in the crowd, dressed in drag with a blond wig and heavy makeup. I made my way through the crush toward him and started to say, "Paolo, you are so beautiful—"

But some guy lurched between us, grabbed Paolo's "breasts," and hollered, "Puttana!—Prostitute!"

An Italian guy pointed to my wine bottle.

"Take it; I don't even know why I have it," I told him.

After a swig, he put the bottle down and said, "Come, let's dance."

While dancing, he asked, "What's your name?"

"Lenore from California."

"Well, Eleonora, I am Gianni."

"Gianni with the curly hair."

"And you are a magic woman."

I burst into laughter. Ha! It felt so good to flirt and dance with somebody. Then, Gianni bent to my ear and whispered an invitation for a drink tomorrow evening. I smiled and accepted.

Suddenly, the music died, and someone hollered, "Let's go!"

The entire party moved en masse into the street.

Stumbling outside, I lost Gianni but joined a motley Mardi Gras parade moving toward the crowded piazza. Someone commandeered a pickup truck, and we hopped aboard the truck bed. As Italian rock music blasted, we danced while slow-rolling down the Corso. At the end of the truck bed, the Pope waved his golden staff, excommunicating sinners left and right.

In the morning, I woke up, rolled over in bed, and stretched without care.

"Oh, wow, what a party!" I said to no one.

Then, I recalled that, amid the frivolities, I'd agreed to meet Gianni for a drink that evening. He was nice. Was I starting to feel safer around men?

Later, I found myself with Gianni at a bar near the piazza, sipping Negronis.

"You've never had a Negroni before?" he asked.

"No, we don't drink them in California."

"Oh, but it is a classic Italian cocktail with gin . . . and sweet vermouth and Campari. It is a blend of the bitter, the sweet, and the aromatic."

"Just like life."

"You know," he said.

After two rounds, I stood up. "I must go home. School is tomorrow."

"Of course. Can I drive you?"

Things went south fast inside Gianni's car parked on a random side street. Pulling me close, he tried to rush me into sex, saying, "Come on, you are so beautiful."

I cut him off. "No, no, not tonight." My anger flared, and I grabbed my purse.

He kept persisting, and I kept resisting. Incensed with anger, I shouted, "Jesus! What are you doing? No!"

Show some respect!

I jumped out of his car and walked home, ending an evening more bitter than sweet.

The next day, I told Lina, one of my Italian girlfriends, about Gianni. She knew of him through her big brother.

"Oh, he has a girlfriend in Bari," she said.

"Of course he does," I said, dripping with sarcasm. *God, what's with these Italian guys?* Bothered, frustrated, and scared of going out again, I wanted to stay away from them.

One afternoon weeks later, I went to Lina and Stefania's family apartment for a hot bath, my favorite pastime on cold-water days. Sitting with wet hair and reading *TIME* magazine in the kitchen, I was minding my own business when Lina and Stefania's gorgeous older brother, Alessandro, walked in. He ignored me as he fixed himself a salami sandwich.

Suddenly, he placed a salami sandwich in front of me. Surprised, I looked up at his smile, and said, "Thank you. You'd make a great wife."

He laughed. Tall and well-dressed, he was seldom home as a band musician. He kept a low profile and seemed very mature.

That night, he called to invite me to a private club to drink and dance.

Wow! I was flattered. Since I knew his lovely sisters, I figured he was nice, too. At the very least, he'd behave himself.

So I said yes. Then, I raced around my room, giggling and changing clothes before he beeped his mini Fiat 500 below my window.

At the club, after some wine, he seemed charmed by me on the dance floor, grinning as I sang along to hit songs in Italian and English. Romantically, he slowly danced me toward the back of the club and into a private room. To the faint beat of the music, we sipped more wine and kissed on a low couch.

All of a sudden, he kissed me hard, too hard, and pushed me down, flattening me into the cushions.

A memory of Gul ripped through my gut, and panic took hold.

Laying atop me, Alessandro grinded against my thigh though we were still dressed. It took forever to shove him off me, yet he refused to stop until he climaxed. Then, without a word, he stood up to signal our departure and drove me home in silence.

Drowning in disgust, I curled into bed. *That motherfucker. He used me for sexual gratification and then tossed me away.*

Alessandro never liked me—he only wanted me for sex. Maybe I'd been too trusting too soon. Or maybe some guys just aren't nice like their sisters. I refused to see this as my fault.

Didn't I deserve respect from boys? Why did I have to shove them off me?

I punched my pillow in anger and pulled my blanket close to my face—everything was so messed up. I snapped off my light.

I never heard from Alessandro again.

I wondered if Stefania and Lina should know the truth about their brother, how he used me to get off. But what good would that have done? And I didn't want them to know how much he had hurt me. I could never have risked upsetting them; I truly cared for them, especially after they had helped me, along with Chiara, to navigate my Italian life by joining me to inspect the nun's dorm and helping me find a new pension room. If telling them meant losing their friendship, I wouldn't have been able to bear it. So

I stayed quiet and let it go, just like I'd stayed quiet about my subterranean wounds to my parents or the police. Lying low, I believed, remained the best course of action.

Before Italy, I never expected to fend off men forcing themselves on me in dim cars or secluded rooms. It made me wonder why I should keep dating if this would only happen again and again. No more men!

They were useless to me.

My IUD was also useless, and I wanted to remove it. It had only protected me from pregnancy, not sexual violence.

One afternoon after class, I joined Chiara, Stefania, and Lina on the cathedral steps. I shifted uncomfortably on the marble, wondering how to ask them for help with this intensely private problem.

"Your haircut looks great," said Chiara.

On a whim, I'd gone to a random hair salon and asked the stylist to cut my long, straight hair short, which brought out natural curls. I didn't tell the stylist I craved a change because seeking romantic adventures had taken a toll on me. In my mirror, I saw a woman with dull eyes, a woman consumed with loathing for the men who only wanted her for sex.

The buzz of a sputtering Vespa scooter cut the air.

"Oh, look at Matteo," said Stefania, pointing to the Vespa driver as he wrangled his scooter around Piazza Quattro Novembre's fountain below. Once it ran smoothly, students stood up and cheered his victory lap.

"I need your help," I said finally. "I'm not dating anymore, and I've got to find a doctor, someone who can remove my IUD."

"A what?" Stefania asked.

I stumbled over my Italian explanation as their eyes grew wide.

"We have never heard of it," Lina said.

"Really? It's this . . . *thing* . . . doctors insert it—" I pointed to my crotch. "And I don't have to take birth control pills."

"And this works?" Chiara said, eyes wide.

I nodded as they pondered in silence. "Well, what do you guys use?" I asked.

They shifted, uncomfortable, until Stefania spoke. "We can't get birth control, never."

"You foreigners are lucky," added Lina. "You can show the pharmacist your passports and get it."

"Wait, so Italian women can't get birth control *or* an abortion *or* a divorce? But *prostitution* is legal?"

"It's like that," said Lina with a shrug.

Chiara said she had endured a back-alley abortion at sixteen.

Now, I was struck silent. I knew nineteen-year-old Lina lived with her toddler Ricci in her parents' apartment, but I didn't know her story.

And I knew that the beauteous firefly Farfalla, extraordinary and clever, transformed barriers against sex into transactional exchanges.

"A doctor will not help you," said Chiara.

I slumped.

"But we'll go to the clinic," she continued. "I have a friend who is a medical student. He can help you, and we'll be your translators."

Later, as I was walking home from the clinic, a random guy shouted at me, "Come on, baby, you sleep with me!"

My gut wrenched. I ignored him. No wonder Italian guys rushed me into bed. Unlike Italian girls, sexually free American girls protected themselves against pregnancy, which prevented the scandal of conceiving an illegitimate child or the inconvenience of paying a prostitute. And this created an open season on American girls.

When I arrived home, my landlady met me at her mailbox and

handed me a letter. I recognized Jackson's handwriting, and with an excited squeal, I scrambled up three flights to my room. As I ripped the envelope open, something glided onto the terrazzo floor. With a gasp, I picked up his pencil sketch of the view of Mount Tamalpais from his Sausalito home.

Oh, Mount Tam. Home.

I set this treasure aside to read about Jackson enduring the rah-rah jocks in his dorm and writing difficult philosophical papers in French. I placed the envelope in the stack of other letters on my desk, noticing how infrequent they had become, as had mine to him. As a lone motorcycle buzzed below my window, I sat with a cold ache in my chest, missing his devotion, wishing I could crawl naked into bed with him at that very moment, sheltered by his love. I closed my eyes to recall my life with Jackson— fun, reckless, and adventurous. For over two years, he had always acted as a gentleman and showed me respect.

Now, we'd drifted apart. Jackson was so far away . . .

I met Jackson on a sun-washed day in May. At seventeen, I had just graduated from my Catholic high school, feeling a heady mix of freedom and anticipation for my graduation trip to Baja California. My life appeared before me, wide open, unformed, and full of possibility.

On that day, a friend had dragged me to Sausalito to "go see a guy." I didn't know much about him or why I agreed to tag along, but that afternoon held a lazy kind of magic, and I felt up for anything.

We approached a house, its entrance draped in thick, purple wisteria that smelled faintly of honey and springtime. A guy about our age stood with his back to us, barefoot in faded jeans, watering roses.

"Hey, where's your brother?" my friend asked, breaking the quiet.

As he turned, an awkward bashfulness took hold of me. His blue shirt hung open to the sun, and his face, framed by longish brown hair, was striking—like a Renaissance youth in those old paintings. Something about him drew me in with a magnetism I couldn't understand.

"He's inside," he said casually as he returned to watering roses.

The way the brother stood, relaxed and self-assured, made me both curious and a little shy.

When my friend's love interest appeared, I followed the two of them inside through glass doors. Then, in a flurry of whispers and giggles, they clattered down a set of wooden stairs and disappeared. I was left standing alone, unsure of what to do with myself, feeling like an unwanted guest.

I shifted awkwardly in the living room, my gaze wandering to the glittering view of Richardson Bay beyond, all blue water and white sails. Instead of soaking in the beauty, all I could think about was how stranded I felt. *Why did I even come here?*

When the rose waterer came inside, I sank onto the couch, trying to mask my embarrassment with indifference.

"They went downstairs," I mumbled, gesturing vaguely toward the stairs.

He didn't seem bothered. "I'm getting some water," he said. "Want some?"

"Sure," I said, grateful for the excuse to follow him.

In the kitchen, dappled sunlight streamed through the windows, catching the faint sheen of water droplets on his arms. He handed me a glass, his smile lighting up his face as he leaned casually against the counter.

"I'm Lenore, by the way."

"I'm Jackson," he said.

A spark of recognition lit in me. "Wait—I know who you are. I've heard about you from David Salvato. He said you guys were best friends before he graduated."

He laughed softly, warm and unguarded. "Oh yeah, David. He's still around, huh?"

We fell into an easy rhythm of conversation, standing by the refrigerator like we'd done it a hundred times before. Every glance, every small smile, made me like him more. There was something so natural about him, so unforced. I wanted to stay in that moment forever.

God, I could really fall for this guy. But he didn't ask for my number, and I was too shy to offer it. The thought of his rejection stung me before it could even happen. What if he didn't want it? Was I imagining the connection between us?

A sudden racket interrupted us as my friend and the other brother came bounding back upstairs, laughing loudly. Their jarring presence broke whatever fragile thread had begun to form between Jackson and me.

"Well, gotta go," I said reluctantly, my voice tinged with disappointment.

Jackson's gaze lingered on me for a moment before he smiled lightly. "Yeah, see you around."

His casual tone stung more than I wanted to admit. Was that all this was? I hesitated, willing myself to say something—anything—but the words stuck in my throat.

Aching with the weight of a missed opportunity, I walked outside, leaving Jackson behind. During my few moments with him, something inside me shifted and I'd fallen hard for him.

Jackson and I got together later in the typical manner of our tribe—over a pot deal. My girlfriend mentioned he was selling some, and I immediately asked her to give him my number. I didn't need any marijuana—I needed to see him again.

The thought of Jackson having my number sent an electric thrill through me; I liked him so much that my longing for us to become boyfriend and girlfriend was all-consuming. He was different from anyone

I'd met, and the idea of him at my side while we explored new adventures filled me with a breathless kind of hope. Maybe, with him, I'd never feel lonely.

We met after school on a sprawling lawn at Tamalpais High, the air tinged with the earthy, woodsy aroma of nearby redwoods. We sat cross-legged in the grass, the sunlight playing through the clouds above us, as we exchanged money and marijuana.

He didn't leave right away, and relief and anticipation swirled inside me. He stayed. He *wanted* to stay. We began to talk, and our conversation flowed so naturally that I hardly noticed how much time had passed. Our words and laughter lifted me on an inviting current.

When we discovered we were born just a month apart, I couldn't stop smiling. He was so nice. Genuine. With some shyness there too, like me. That softness in him only made him more magnetic, drawing me further into his orbit.

I kept waiting for him to ask to see me again. Did he feel the same attraction? Or was I just imagining it?

The late afternoon sun began to sink behind the hills, casting shadows across the lawn. Still, I didn't want this moment to end. I could've sat there with him forever, losing myself in his handsome face, his warm laughter, and the way his eyes crinkled when he smiled. It was as though the world had softened around us, becoming more beautiful by our being together.

Finally, Jackson stood, brushing bits of grass from his jeans. My heart sank slightly, knowing our time together was ending, but he smiled that wide grin of his and said, "Well, I've got to head home. We should go hiking on Mount Tam sometime. We can hike down into Muir Woods from the Mountain Home Inn."

My breath caught. He did want to see me again. "Oh, yeah, I'd like that," I said, trying to sound as casual as I could despite bursting with hope.

"All right," he said, his tone easy, like it was the simplest thing in the world. "I'll call you. It's going to be a great summer."

Then he hugged me, and I melted into him, loving the solid feel of his arms around me. For a moment, everything felt perfect. All was well in my world.

As he walked away, I watched him until he disappeared from view. The redwoods swayed slightly in the breeze, their whispers mingling with my racing thoughts. *Will he really call me? Is this the beginning of something real that lasts?*

For now, I let myself believe, let myself dream.

Over the summer, we couldn't spend much time together. I left on my three-week graduation trip to Baja, and when I got back, Jackson had already left for a month in Paris with his family. So, we traded ardent letters, sharing our favorite books and our mutual love of being in nature.

From Mexico, I wrote to him about how the soft, humid air felt on my skin. From Paris, he wrote about drunks lying "in heaps, wearing filthy clothes that hid bottles of wine."

He masked his affection for me by shyly writing in French: "Tu es vraiment spéciale," which I translated: "You are really special."

By August, we fell into each other so easily, excited to spend as much time together as possible. Now a luminous girl in love, I loved going with him to parties or watching foreign films with him in San Francisco art houses. I loved how he drew in my journal like Da Vinci and wrote about how much I enchanted him. I loved how he spoke French with Mom's Haitian cleaning lady. And I loved how, on a hike, we heard Santana rehearsing in a house in the trees below.

I had found a kind and devoted boyfriend; we never had fights or drama.

Freed from a Catholic uniform after twelve long years, I listened to

Jackson's questions about my high school. "What? You've never read Kafka's *Metamorphosis*?"; "You didn't study M.C. Escher in your art class?"; "Wait, you want to be a writer and never read Camus? *The Stranger* is so good!"

Well-read and worldly, Jackson also knew the coolest places to explore. Alongside this adventurer, I experienced a sweat session inside an authentic replica of an Indigenous sweat lodge hidden in a forest near Muir Woods.

Once, Jackson took me on a night hike, leading me up a forested trail to a platform above Mill Valley's twinkling lights.

"Beautiful," I said. When I turned to him, he was already looking at me.

"Yes, beautiful," he said, and he kissed me passionately under a full moon.

On my most memorable birthday, a rare winter snowfall transformed Mount Tamalpais; we wandered through an ethereal wonderland of snow-dusted fire roads and twisted chaparral covered by a delicate layer of white.

When his sister's marriage to a member of Quicksilver Messenger Service and Jefferson Starship got him backstage passes to concerts at the Winterland Ballroom, Jackson and I stood in the shadows with rock gods. I had landed worlds away from the confining corridors of Catholic school. As the backstage resounded with humming amplifiers and electric energy, it struck me: this was more than rebellion. It was transformation. And that felt like real magic.

But Jackson also carried a dangerous appeal. He was a bad boy. One Friday night, as he waited for me to get ready, he sat at our piano and played Schumann with effortless grace, a gram of cocaine tucked in his wallet.

The following summer, I helped Jackson plant and tend his lush rooftop marijuana plantation, an illicit cargo thriving in manure he had collected on Horse Hill. Being stupid teenagers, we posed, proud and naïve, for snapshots among illegal plants as tall as trees. By harvest time, every plant had disappeared.

One evening about a week later, Jackson grabbed a fat stack of bills from his desk drawer, his face aglow with triumph.

"All gone. All sold."

"Wow, that was fast. How much is that?"

"A thousand bucks." Good money for a summer job in those days.

"Holy shit, we gotta celebrate! Let's go to Mamounia, that Moroccan restaurant in the City."

"Let's go right now!" said my partner in crime.

After speeding across the Golden Gate Bridge, we dined on a lavish

Beyond Mount Tamalpias, I naively posed with illegal marijuana atop Jackson's roof.
© Lenore Greiner 1973, edited 2022.

feast under a tented ceiling, eating with our fingers and lounging on silken pillows. When our French-Moroccan waiter handed the underaged Jackson a wine list, I twisted my cloth napkin. He ordered a fine French wine and sat back on our pillows, radiant with victory.

I cherished how full of life he was, how vibrant and fun.

"Robed and red-capped waiters served us like a sultan and his bride," he wrote in my journal later about our royal night out. "Truly an evening to remember, one quite worthy of a deserving Lenore."

That was a crazy, renegade time in Marin, I thought, sitting in my pension room with Jackson's letter in my hand.

Then, I remembered one special afternoon during our first summer together.

After hiking mountain trails, we had warmed up before a fire at Jackson's house during a typical, chilly Marin County summer. As Jackson practiced on the grand piano, I sprawled on the Persian carpet under the piano, reading and reveling in my comfortable, beautiful new life.

As the last notes he played lingered in the air, Jackson stood up, came to me, encircled me in his arms, and led me upstairs to explore another undiscovered terrain. In his elfin room, a reading nook sheltered a narrow bed beneath a window framing the oaks outside. There, I savored his smell and felt his breath upon my skin as I drifted into a dream state from his soft kisses. I ran my hands from his naked shoulders down his sweaty back as we were washed away, buoyant upon the waves of our own open sea, rolling together.

"Lenore," he whispered. "Lenore."

Jackson was my first love. We told each other we'd be together forever once I returned from Italy.

Was coming to Italy a big mistake? Maybe I should've gone right to Berkeley instead of deferring for a year. Then, I could've been with Jackson this whole time. Did my choice ruin us?

Yet at the time, I was thrilled to embark on my year abroad, a serendipitous gift of adventure and learning. I wasn't the type to let any guy stand in my way despite loving Jackson to death. Besides, Jackson had said, "Of course, you *have* to go."

A rising feeling of loss clenched my throat as I fought back tears. I rarely thought about Jackson these days, distracted by my new confusing life, but that night I missed him so much I ached.

With a huge sigh, I placed his letter atop a stack of my letters from home. Then, I slit open the envelope of Mom's latest letter.

My hands trembled as I read her words, which made the blood rush into my face.

Mom had transferred my application from UC Berkeley to UC Davis because "Grace and I visited Davis, and we think it's nicer."

Damn it! I put her letter down, shaking my head in disbelief. So she *had* wanted to separate Jackson and me by sending me to Italy. And now she'd made sure I'd never go to Berkeley.

If my parents knew the worst thing to ever happen to me happened in Italy, would they feel differently? How was feeling scared and getting assaulted in Italy better than feeling safe and in love in Berkeley near Jackson? It wasn't. But there was nothing I could do about it because I was not going to tell my parents anything.

I crumpled her letter and then smoothed it out and placed it upon my stack, knowing each missive documented my year abroad.

Exhausted by my heavy emotions, I pushed my chair away from my table. Standing up heavily, I taped Jackson's sketch of Mount Tamalpais to my wall and stared at this memento of my once magnificent life. Memories of home pulled on me.

If I hadn't left Jackson, left for Italy, I wouldn't have been raped.

This painful reality left me craving an escape. I wanted to time-travel back to my life before Italy when I was dancing around with Jackson or lying naked in his arms, happy, loved, blissfully unaware of the profound loss of innocence awaiting me on another continent.

I recalled a faraway memory of the September night before I left for Italy. Jackson held me, his eyes soft with sadness, and said, "I'm going to miss you."

"Don't forget about me."

Grinning, he said, "Never. And you—don't end up a slave in a Tunisian harem."

Recalling his well-timed wit, I let out a loud belly laugh for the first time in a long time. In that moment, the weight on my heart lifted, if only briefly. I wasn't naïve—I knew things wouldn't change overnight. But for now, laughter let me breathe.

14

RESILIENCE

I ran into Missy from Maryland in the piazza. She said of her roommate, "Ann's gone home."

"What?" I said, shocked. "Why?"

"Yeah, yesterday. We went down to the train station to help her catch the rapido to Rome." She pulled her overcoat against the winter wind. "She just gave up. You know how she hated it here, how she struggled with Italian."

"Yeah, I feel bad for her. But maybe it was a good choice for her."

We walked down Corso Vannucci, arm in arm. The sun shined as Fiats tangled and untangled themselves in the streets, and the wind flapped the vivid magazine covers on the newsstands.

Though I felt bone-tired, I refused to retreat like Ann. I straightened my posture and carried on, priding myself on my resilience.

I had shut down emotionally and stayed silent, shoving my awful memories underground. And I was *not* going home. But I wished I could take a break from Perugia.

Ann no longer our concern, we changed the topic.

"So, where are we going for spring break?" asked Missy.

I burst into laughter. She had just asked the right question. Had she been reading my mind?

"Look at our schedule," said Missy, pulling a paper from her backpack. "We have two weeks off between our second and third Italian courses. Right around Easter, like a spring break."

Grinning at her, I danced around her. The idea of leaving Umbria's dank skies behind for two weeks in the Grecian sun felt intoxicating.

Later, my afternoon class got unruly, which often happened when we recited complex verb conjugations. A wave of restlessness rippled across the rows of our long desks. Stifled guffaws broke out. Wearing leather jackets, Gul and his roommate sat below me a few rows, and next to me sat two staid Swiss girls who were shooting spitballs at their necks.

After a satisfying direct hit, the roommate turned around and asked, "Che cosa—What?"

Bent over their notebooks with sly smiles, the Swiss girls ignored him. My shoulders shuddered.

Good God, it might not just be me. Are the Swiss girls victims, too?

15

REBELS WITHOUT A CLUE

Missy from Maryland was a bad influence, but I welcomed her rebellious-ness because it distracted me from my loneliness.

In early April, I went to Missy's place for a hot bath. Afterward, I joined her in the kitchen, combing my wet hair and covering my coughs. Despite visiting a doctor and taking antibiotics, my stubborn, painful bronchitis still hung on for dear life.

Excitedly, we planned our trip. I said, "We should fly to Athens from Rome."

"That costs too much," said Missy.

She bent forward to make a dangerous suggestion. "Why don't we skip the train from Perugia to Ancona? We can hitchhike there to catch our train south to the port?"

"Hitchhiking? That's downright dangerous," I said, biting my nails.

Stealing toilet paper or food could have resulted in arrests or getting sent home packing. But hitchhiking?

"Missy, we could get kidnapped or raped or murdered. Aren't you scared? Because I am. It's too risky."

"Well, I calculate the odds as low," she said as her blue eyes peered at me through her gold-tinged curls. She seemed unconcerned, but she had no idea where I'd come from—I had never told her how I suffered every day after getting raped. How it ruined my year abroad. Even though a break from Perugia was a godsend, it wouldn't relieve the pain of sitting in class with that asshole all semester.

I didn't know how much longer I could stand seeing him, month after month. And I didn't know how much more disrespect I could take from creepy Italian guys.

Do I continue living in this dangerous place? Or kill my Italian dream and leave Perugia? And go where? I can't go home—I couldn't bear Mom's interrogations about leaving early. But isn't my Italian dream already dead?

I rubbed my temples with my fingers, feeling so broken inside I couldn't think right anymore as Missy kept bugging me about saving money by hitchhiking.

When her insistence became too much to handle, I shrugged weakly and agreed.

So the following morning, we stood, freezing on a road outside town, hitchhiking, which the Italians called autostopping.

Soon, two Italian guys pulled over, and I scrutinized them. They seemed okay, especially since they appeared to be high schoolers.

After they enthusiastically agreed to drive us to Ancona via the autostrada, we squished into the back seat. Missy and I smiled at each other. We had just saved tons of lire that would be better spent on ouzo in a taverna on Crete.

As the car rolled on, I caught an odd exchange of glances between the two guys.

Stiff with fear, I kept my eyes on them, watching, waiting for what they'd do or say next. And fighting the urge to brain Missy for her dangerous idea.

The car wound through the Umbrian hills, taking too long to reach the autostrada.

What the hell? We were out in the boonies. This wasn't right. "Is this the way to Ancona?" I asked.

"Oh, yes, yes. We're taking a shortcut."

"So, when do we get on the autostrada?"

"Soon." The driver kept his eyes on the road.

My stomach turned.

"Relax," Missy said. "Just let him drive."

How could she be so calm at a time like this when we were clearly about to be kidnapped? Minutes passed until the driver abruptly turned up a steep, one-lane road ascending a forested hill. I breathed slowly, telling myself everything was going to be okay. But my adrenaline spiked, and anxious thoughts surged through my mind.

God damn it! Why'd I let Missy talk me into this?

Feeling claustrophobic in the back seat, I exchanged a knowing look with Missy; she gestured to the hairdryer sticking out of her bag—a potential defense weapon.

The driver stopped before a dilapidated stone farmhouse and turned to face us.

"Now," he said, "we are going to go inside and make love."

Oh, hell no!

"No, we get out," Missy said in her broken Italian.

I commanded in Italian, "No! Let us out. Now!"

The two guys traded looks as if our refusals were useless. We didn't know what they had planned.

"Listen," said Missy, jabbing her index finger at them. "My father is a good friend of President Ford."

They traded alarmed looks.

President Ford? I thought.

With all my strength, I pushed on the back of the front passenger seat, screaming, "Let us out! Open the door!"

The passenger opened his door and got out. I couldn't jump out fast enough with Missy right behind me.

We ran at full speed away from the car, trundling our bags, slipping and sliding down a steep hill on wet grass and mud. We ran and ran as our feet sank into heavy muck and a cold wind whipped us. Our former captors called us back, but we couldn't understand them. We didn't care.

As my heart pounded, I spied an empty country road below. Once on the roadside, we stopped to catch our breath. I seethed inside. This was turning out to be some spring break. I couldn't even get out of fucking Perugia without getting threatened.

"Shit, Missy, what the fuck just happened?"

"Jesus H. Christ," she said.

"We almost got *raped,* Missy. No more autostopping."

We needed to find a bus stop, so we started down the road.

"Hey, does your father really know President Ford?" It could be possible. Missy *was* from Maryland.

"No, I just said that."

"Well, it worked." I filed that tactic away in my mind along with another practical use for my hair dryer.

We marched on. The wind pushed at our backs as we walked through a silent yet idyllic countryside, passing farms and pastures. After our break to freedom, exhaustion overtook me, and my feet dragged. I was so tired of feeling tired.

A guttural wail pierced the stillness—raw, unearthly, and never-ending. The hair on the nape of my neck stiffened.

Once it stopped, a farmer walked out of a barn's wide entrance, his tall rubber boots caked in filth, carrying two sloshing buckets. Blood spilled over the rims, staining the muddy ground.

That sound, sharp and unrelenting, had struck a deep nerve. *Did he just slaughter an animal?*

Was that how it felt to be led to slaughter? Vulnerable, unsuspecting, betrayed by the very ground you trusted to hold you steady? Italy had a way of turning the tables, flipping safety into peril, like some cruel joke.

No one had ever warned me about rape. Not once.

Now, I knew better—or should have known better. Yet, like a lamb, too trusting, I had stumbled into danger again with open eyes yet blind to the cost. My shame stung worse than my fear. Why hadn't I refused to hitchhike? I could've kicked myself for my own naïveté, again and again trusting the world to be kind.

We trudged down the roadside. Desperate for normalcy, I asked with a brittle voice, "So, we're taking the train all the way to the port tomorrow?"

"Yeah," Missy said flatly. She now knew how fast life could turn sideways without warning, leaving you stunned in its wake.

The next day, after a train ride down the Adriatic coast, we arrived in Pescara in my maternal ancestral province of Abruzzo.

Exhausted, we spent the night at Mom's cousin's place. A schoolteacher, Madonna had appointed herself as my Italian mother and showered me with kindness. Over the previous Christmas break, she had hosted me, filling me with homemade pasta and fresh market vegetables.

This time, I looked forward to her special minestrone for two weary students.

"My God, this is unbelievable," said Missy, hoovering her meal.

I smiled. Sharing a bit of my family with Missy warmed my heart. For a moment, my loneliness and homesickness eased. *Maybe I should visit Madonna more often*, I thought. *Then I might not feel so cold and alone.*

We arrived in Brindisi the next morning to board a ferry and sail across the Ionian Sea to Athens. In this rough port town, we knew two American girls would attract attention, so we spoke Italian only to endure rude whispers in an indecipherable dialect from raunchy men sidling up to us.

As I followed Missy on a narrow sidewalk, a Vespa scooter sped toward us. With perfect timing, the driver made a bold grab at my breast.

"What the fuck?" I yelled. Shaking with anger, I spun around but found my assailant long gone.

Why is this goddamned country full of aggressive men who only take what they want? A mix of anger and despair made my stomach churn. I was sick to death of feeling powerless, of never feeling safe. I stayed vigilant, always scanning, always bracing—but somehow, it was never enough.

Why did these violations keep happening? What invisible thread kept yanking me back into danger? Was it me? Was I to blame? The question gnawed at the edges of my mind. But how could I be responsible for their actions? For their violence?

16

A FEW GOOD MEN

Trouble started in a ticket office in Athens' port of Piraeus after we bought two third-class round-trip tickets for the night ferry to Crete. When I stepped outside into the sun, tickets in hand, an adrenaline rush ran through me. Tomorrow morning we'd arrive in Agia Galini, a small fishing village on Crete's tantalizing southern coast. Walking to the ferry dock and bursting with hopes for adventure, I picked a flower and placed it in my hair.

"Don't wear that flower," said Missy. "You'll attract too much attention."

I yanked out my flower and threw it on the ground. She was right. What was I thinking? "What the hell, Missy? Why are men such assholes?" I glowered.

"Well, look. Let's just have fun," she said, talking me down. "We'll hang out, eat good food, and get really tan."

"That's the best plan I've heard in a while," I said, smiling. "I can't wait to get there."

Aboard our night ferry, engines rumbled beneath our feet as we headed to the bar. At a table, we joined some backpackers and five bottles of retsina, a cheap white wine infused with pine resin. Amid the scent of salt air and retsina's offensive turpentine smell, we toasted our new friends and celebrated our voyage to Crete.

As the ocean rolled, we listened to those wanderers' tales of European treks, Moroccan mishaps, and overland journeys through Africa. Our more ordinary history surprised them.

"You mean, you stay in Italy and go to school?" one guy asked.

"Yeah," I said. "This is our one getaway before May exams."

A uniformed officer came to our table, punched our tickets, and handed them back to everyone.

Except us.

"Hey, where are our tickets?" I asked.

"These," he said, waving the flimsy, gray papers with Greek lettering, "are not round-trip tickets."

"No, no, they're round-trip tickets, and we need them back," I said, slurring my words.

Our dust-up attracted the captain's attention. A gentleman sporting a trim salt-and-pepper beard and a crisp white shirt topped with blue-and-gold striped epaulets, he listened to his officer's Greek explanation as we watched, balancing our sea legs as the Aegean tossed his vessel.

He turned to me and said, "No, miss. These are two one-way tickets."

"That's not right! We bought round-trip tickets," I said, flush with a bellyful of retsina.

"I can tell you that you paid 200 drachmas each for two one-way tickets," he said in precise English.

My head exploded in confusion. *Oh my God. Not another scam. Jesus, I'm on vacation.* I held my ground, and he stayed adamant.

The captain explained the currency exchange between drachmas and US dollars. Then, Missy and I calculated what we had paid from US dollars to lire to drachmas. Or was it drachmas to lire to US dollars? What exactly did we do?

Tears sprang into my eyes. Missy stared mutely.

Choosing to fight, I said, "I'm positive we bought round-trip tickets."

Our captain fought back. "No, miss. These two one-way tickets," he said in his courtly manner.

I studied the indecipherable tickets. "How would I know? It's all in Greek."

"No, miss, I assure you."

I stood, weaving before him, beating back panic as my heart pounded. If he was right, it meant I wouldn't have enough money to return to Perugia.

Then I made my second miscalculation of the day. I turned to Missy and unleashed my frustration with a corrupt aside using the worst Italian words, a colossal blunder. "What the fuck does he want?"

A stunned silence fell upon him.

"Listen, my dear," he said in perfect Italian.

His words ignited my mortification.

"I cannot help you any further," he said, with much more courtesy than I deserved. He took off for more important duties than dealing with a drunk, mouthy American girl.

I dragged my miserable self to my third-class bunk to lay my spinning head on a pillow stinking of stale vomit, which I deserved.

The next day we landed in Heraklion and rode a local bus to Agia Galini. I sagged next to Missy, nursing my foul hangover and puzzling long and hard over my money situation.

"You okay?"

"I guess so, just silently stewing in my stupidity."

Our bus lumbered past farmer fields dotted with wafts of scarlet red poppies radiant in the spring sun; I opened my window and took a big breath, noticing how much more easily I breathed in Crete's clean air. I calmed down and my mood brightened.

In Agia Galini, a local led us to his hotel. Our clean, all-white double room had a bathroom and a terrace.

"It's only a dollar a night! Can you believe it?" said Missy. "I love it."

"Great," I said. "Maybe my money will last after all."

During two weeks of parties and hangovers, we rambled up steep, white-washed streets adorned with sky-blue doorways. The narrow main street tumbled to a pretty plaza facing the sea and a modest fishing port. The aquamarine Aegean shimmered as the wind blew in from Africa. On a nearby rocky beach, naked, sun-worshipping German tourists lolled.

Village nightlife happened in Bozo's, a seaside taverna awash in retsina and ouzo, a dangerous liquor smelling of licorice. On our first night, we joined backpackers—Brits and Canadians, South Africans and Aussies, and other Americans. Mostly guys, they went by "John from South Africa" or "Seth from Vancouver." This crowd, all strangers in a new town, was especially friendly and well-oiled by retsina and ouzo.

"I'm a Kiwi. Where are youse from?" asked Logie from New Zealand, swaying above our table. His tall shot glass of ouzo threatened to spill on us.

"We're Americans," answered Missy.

"Where're you headed next?" he asked, his blue tank top displaying tanned, well-muscled arms.

"Oh, we have to go back to Italy," I said. "Where we're in school."

"School? Why are you going to school? Why aren't you going around the world?"

"Well, I'd like to, eventually," I answered, looking down, surprised by how shy I suddenly felt.

"Do it now! That's what I'm doing." His enthusiasm for world travel was clear. His eyes glowed, and every word seemed an exclamation of his devotion to adventure.

Then, breaking the topic of conversation, a British girl moaned, "God, I got so pissed last night."

"Why'd you get so mad?" asked an American girl.

"Mad? No, I wasn't mad. I got too drunk."

Pissed meant drunk. Ha! This mob taught me new definitions of English words, which I recorded in my journal. I was always interested in language and words and people and places. This mingling session with people from all over fascinated me and reminded me how much I enjoyed learning about the world.

At tables heavy with bottles, in the interest of international relations, the guys entertained us with Anglo-Saxon slang nicknames for penises: John Thomas, tallywacker, willy, and knob.

In a thick brogue, giant Ewan from Edinburgh announced his as "Vlad the Impaler."

In the wee hours, I ended up with Logie and a couple of young fishermen on their boat, trawling just off the port. We passed around a bottle of ouzo as they laid their nets.

Reflections of the taverna's lights bounced upon the black water, and strains of Joni Mitchell's "California," a song about missing home while wandering Europe, drifted toward us.

I shivered as homesickness swirled through me, and I longed for my old life back home. And for Jackson. *He's a good man.* I wished we weren't growing apart. My last letter to him began, "Ciao! It's about time! Jeez, I thought you had a heart attack or something." He hadn't written since February, two months earlier.

As I saw my former life falling away, I trembled.

Logie placed his coat over my shoulders against the chill, and I smiled my thanks. Once ashore, he insisted on carrying me two blocks to my room against my protestations.

"I can walk. I'm fine!"

"The lady had too much to drink and requires safe passage." He laughed.

He was silly and gentlemanly, a new friend watching out for me. We'd only just met, but I could tell his behavior was genuine. It gave me hope that he was one of the good ones and I wasn't doomed to be repeatedly assaulted for the rest of my life.

The next night, a shirtless, blind drunk Logie entered the taverna. For entertainment, I watched him weave through the bar, leaving a wake of bottles tumbling from the tabletops. As he passed us, his pants dropped to his ankles, and with such excellent timing, I got a face-level view of his John Thomas. Missy and I almost fell off our chairs, paralyzed by laughter.

Malcolm from London rushed over. "Logie, man, yank up your pants!"

"Get away, you bloody Pom!" the Kiwi said, shoving him aside.

He staggered to the bar to order another shot of ouzo. After a swift assessment of Logie, Bozo bounded around his bar to pull up Logie's pants before pouring his drink.

With a bleary grin, Malcolm from London winked at me. "Down the ouzo trail another victim falls."

I never blamed Logie for the unintentional exposure of his John Thomas. After all, it was an admirable feat, circumnavigating the globe dead drunk.

17

A FISTFUL OF LIRE

After sailing back to Italy, Missy and I stood in the Brindisi train station amid the stink of engine fuel. At the ticket window, as we studied the train schedule, I frowned after digging into my purse to find a single 1,000-lire bill.

I gritted my teeth. "I hate not having enough money."

I felt so stupid and incompetent. I had just met kids traveling around the world for a year, and I couldn't even plan a short spring break without a disaster.

"I'm so sorry, Lenore. I only have enough for one ticket home, or I'd lend it to you."

"Thanks, but that's okay," I said. "I have just enough money for a ticket to Ostuni to see my relatives. I have to call my cousin Lucio and let him know. Hope there's a Banco di Roma there to see if my money has arrived."

After buying my ticket on a cheap local train to Ostuni, I saw Missy off on her northbound train. Then, I crossed the tracks to board my train and sit on a hard wooden seat. When my stomach grumbled, I smiled, thinking about how much my relatives adored feeding me. I also shifted with excitement, anticipating my visit to Banco di Roma.

My train lumbered along the Adriatic coast, passing a gray-green plain of olive orchards. I thought about my father's father, Joe Asiano, originally Giuseppe Asciano. At fourteen, he emigrated alone to work with his father Frank, or Francesco, in Ohio's steel mills in Steubenville. After saving money, Joe and his dad sent for Joe's mother and sisters, and that was how my paternal family took root in America.

Outside my window, the province of Apulia, my ancestral landscape, shimmered in the sun. A land of red earth, white stucco buildings, palm trees, and a sea of unbelievably crystalline waters raced by.

Is this where we come from? It didn't look like Italy at all but like the Middle East in my Catholic schoolbooks or Dad's *TIME* magazines.

How could my paternal grandfather leave such a beautiful land? I wondered. Crushing poverty drove him away when he was only fourteen. What guts he must've had, leaving everything behind for an unknown future.

Remembering my letter from Arcangelo, my maternal grandfather, I marveled at their bravery. Again, I saw myself standing on the shoulders of my ancestors.

If they overcame formidable obstacles, I could also find the guts to beat my miseries in Perugia: my sadness, woundedness, and loneliness—even my bronchitis, which had hung on after two weeks on Crete. Instead of living amid fear and danger, I could stay strong and keep moving forward.

Ostuni appeared in my window, breaking my reverie, and I stood up to get a good look. Famous as The White City, the white-washed town of twisting, narrow streets gleamed in the sun and resembled a Greek village. In ancient times, Ostuni was part of Magna Graecia like much of southern

Italy. During the Middle Ages, control by the Byzantine Empire reinforced its Greek architecture.

As soon as I descended from my train, my paternal relatives smothered me affectionately and promptly took me home for pranzo, the main afternoon meal. They placed a mountain of handmade stacciodde, the regional pasta, before me, watching with wide grins as I inhaled it like a starving wolf.

"Eleonora," they announced, "We are taking you on a tour to show you the land your family sold to get to America. Lucio! We're taking your car!"

In Lucio's Lancia sedan, we rode around Ostuni's old quarter, which was appropriately dubbed "The Wedding Cake," with its steep white streets layered like a sugary confection. I adored it—it even cheered me up more than the stacciodde.

Then, we sped down one-lane country roads, past olive orchards bordered by miles of stone walls. In the sunset's slanting shadows, we pulled over at a stony patch of land where a sad olive grove stood. It was once my peasant ancestors' only source of wealth.

And it was another reminder of my family's strength. I came from solid stock. Solid, crazy, pasta-loving stock.

Surely, I could handle anything life threw at me. I saw so much beauty in the world, so much deliciousness. I had to try to focus on that instead of fear and danger. I had to be strong and keep moving forward.

The next day, on a lovely southern Italian spring morning, I walked to Banco di Roma in hopes that my money had arrived.

"There isn't any," said the teller.

My stomach sank. I'd heard this before, when I first arrived in Perugia. How could there be no money? I slumped against the counter. "But when's it coming?" I asked.

The teller shrugged. "No one can say, Signorina."

I walked outside and started down the sidewalk through the main piazza. How was I going to get back to Perugia? What was I supposed to do? Talk about feeling unsafe. The idea of being out here all alone with no resources terrified me. I had family here, yes. But spending a day with them didn't mean I knew them well enough to ask for money. Besides, I'd die of embarrassment.

I could've called home but didn't feel up for a Mom upbraiding. I had to get back. I had classes to attend, life to live, and a future to plan. *Jesus.* When would my luck change? When would my fabulous year abroad be about anything other than constant sickness and trouble?

When I returned to my relatives' home dejected, I kept my situation to myself.

Strangely, one of the elders pulled me aside. He stuffed enough money in my pocket for a train ticket to Perugia. For that fistful of lire, I threw my arms around him in tears, overwhelmed with gratitude. When I was a kid, older Italian relatives liked to slip me cash, saying, "Now, don't tell your parents."

And I wouldn't. This was between Italy and me. This was about luck, fate, and receiving an ounce of good fortune after a series of missteps.

Traveling up the Adriatic coast, I had just enough time to stop in Pescara to visit Madonna. She happily prepared for us an excellent midday meal of homemade pasta and fresh produce from the farmer's market. After we ate in her warm, sunny apartment, she sat silently over her espresso as an endless coughing fit grabbed me.

"You cannot go back to Perugia," she said. "You are too sick."

"I have to. My third course of Italian starts on Monday," I rasped between gasps for air. "Or I won't get my Italian certificate."

As a schoolteacher, she understood, yet she knitted her brows as I coughed into my napkin.

"Do you need that certificate for your university back in America?"

"Davis? No, it's just a supplementary thing. For extra credit."

"Ah," she said. "Not a requirement for your college. You are too sick to go back. You can stay here and get better. We will call your parents."

Without a way to reimburse her, I twisted my hands. "Madonna, no. It's too expensive to call them."

As I sagged in my dining chair, she picked up her phone and, with great kindness, initiated a conversation with my parents as I translated. She repeated my dire symptoms, louder and louder, until Mom and Dad consented and thanked Madonna.

"It's nothing. The ocean air will do her good," said Madonna. "She can stay here. Grace, too, when she comes to Italy after graduation."

Madonna hung up, clapped her hands, and said, "Ecco, fatto—There, done."

I gave her a big hug as a vast, surprising sigh left me. With my lungs rebelling in my chest, I could escape Perugia and free myself from those gray, oppressive skies. And I'd no longer live amid constant reminders of that horrible night, including Gul sitting in my class day after day.

I had been living in denial, unable to understand why my bronchitis hung on. Now, a literal illness gave me an excuse to face the truth.

The next morning, I caught a train to Perugia to notify my school, pack my stuff, and say sad goodbyes to my closest friends, Missy, Paolo, and my Italian girlfriends. I'd miss everyone terribly yet had no regrets about leaving. All along, I hadn't wanted to leave Perugia until now. Madonna gave me an important reason, my health. She had no idea my departure would help my mental health too. This wasn't me giving up. This was me accepting it was time to free myself from Italy's only land-locked province. This was me beginning to heal.

Madonna greeted me at the train station with a registered letter from Dad.

"Oh, no. Now what?" I said.

She watched me open the envelope holding a check to reimburse Madonna for her expensive call to California. I also opened a note he'd scribbled on his professional stationery, ordering me to "get in that Adriatic sun and bake out your lungs."

I loved Dad so much. Tears spilled from my eyes. *He* was also proof that good men existed.

Quivering with sadness, I knew I could never break his heart by revealing I had been raped alone in Italy. Not only did I want to evade blame—my intuition constantly whispered that my parents would blame me—but also, I couldn't deal with causing Dad the pain that would come with knowing I'd suffered.

No, it was better to let sleeping dogs lie.

At first, at Madonna's, I slept almost around the clock as if I hadn't slept for months. When I did awaken, I'd find a sunny spring day outside.

I spent my time alone while Madonna taught at school. I relaxed, snacked, napped, and read Italian gossip rags and fashion magazines. I savored the peace, yet sadness dogged me. I began letters home and then tossed them out. Once, I picked up my journal, wrote down the word "malaise," and then put it down.

Madonna intuitively knew I needed to rest; she had no idea how much. Solitary in her quiet home while she was off teaching, I decompressed from my chaos in Perugia: getting sick, making bad decisions, stealing food, and hitchhiking. I'd tried to put a Band-Aid on it all by indulging in my social life and friends' companionship, escaping to Crete, and abandoning my studies by clubbing every night. Everything that had kept me in denial had helped me survive, but it had also made me sick.

Madonna's kindness offered me a new life near the restorative sea. I fell into the open arms of relatives and family friends in Abruzzo. I joined in their raucous family meals. I went to the beach with them for days in sun and water. On Sundays, we took drives into Abruzzo's mountains, visiting my maternal grandmother's hometown, Sulmona, and my grandfather Arcangelo's birthplace, Introdacqua.

My mood lightened. Everywhere I looked, summer hinted at its arrival. Roses exploded from their vines. Luscious gelato cones accompanied Italians on their afternoon walks. Tractors cleaned the sand at the beach clubs as workers set up battalions of lounges and umbrellas that popped up in rows like multi-colored mushrooms.

For the first time in a long time, I felt . . . happy. But I was impatient, too, eagerly awaiting Grace's arrival. I missed her, and I missed speaking English.

On a beach walk one morning, I met two Americans my age, a guy and a girl passing out flyers.

"What's this about?" I asked in English, taking one.

"It's a newsletter with good news," said the guy.

I recognized the masthead: "Bambini di Dio." I knew the Children of God from their flyers plastered around the College of Marin, all written by Mo, the leader of a Jesus cult.

"Oh, you've heard of us?"

"Oh, yeah, back home."

"Where?"

I took a step back, not wanting to encourage them. Something felt off in my gut. "In California."

I listened to their story. Backpacking around Europe, they'd met these incredible people in Rome, and now, here they were, living by the sea and doing God's work.

"Hey, it'd be cool if you came over for dinner. Our apartment is a short walk from here," said the girl with a wide smile.

Hiding my bemused smile, I accepted their invitation to a midday meal. I had the time, and my curiosity got the better of me. Hearing their come-on to join their cult certainly would be entertaining. Besides, I was alone all day while my relatives worked, and one meal with Americans couldn't hurt. So I spontaneously took on this adventure, knowing they'd never win me over.

I soon found myself crowded at a table in a tight kitchen with more Children of God, Italian and American.

Shifting on my hard chair, I picked at their lukewarm canned pasta served in cheap plastic bowls, which depressed me. Sensing a weird energy, I looked around the table, puzzled. The others looked and acted like a family yet displayed an emotional flatness. They were very different from my relatives, who enjoyed a raucous conviviality that flowed during our family meals.

My eyes darted about the dingy kitchen. What were the relationships here? Who was married to whom? And who did these random children belong to?

A sudden intuition grabbed me, screaming inside, *Get out of here.* I jumped off my chair, perhaps too fast, and all eyes turned to me, which was the last thing I wanted.

"I hate to be rude"—I picked up my purse—"but I've got to get back to my cousin's now."

"Oh, no," said an older guy. "Sure you can't stay until tonight? We're playing a concert in the piazza. We've got a great rock band."

"Sorry, no. Gotta go."

So that was how they did it. *Stay for the rock concert, and tomorrow, there'll be something else fun to do. And, before you know it, you're entangled in a cult, and two years have gone by.*

I slipped out the door and bounced down the stairs to the street; I figured I'd never make a great cult member—I liked my freedom too much. The ability to escape when I needed to felt like an instinct woven into me. But looking into their smiling faces during our meal unsettled me. How easy it could've been to get pulled into something dangerous when loneliness, pain, or vulnerability gnawed at you long enough. When even the most rigid rules could've felt like protection, the most suffocating control seemed like care. If I had stayed in Perugia, if the wrong voice had whispered at the right moment, could that have been me?

But not now. I felt my strength returning. And with it came a quiet peace from knowing I no longer needed to be saved by anyone but myself.

I rushed to the warmth of true family within Madonna's home. Grateful for her maternal care and delicious meals ending with chats over espresso, I treasured living with her near the beach, and the safety and comfort lifted my spirits.

The day of Grace's arrival, I paced inside Rome's air terminal, overseen by Uzi-toting soldiers, my eyes searching for my little sister.

When Grace finally appeared from customs, I ran to her. "I can't believe you're here!" I encircled her in a huge hug.

"I'm totally burned out," she said.

The same little spitfire, my sister hadn't changed at all. Yet her expression told me I had.

I knew she saw my outward changes: the short curly hair, the Italian clothes, and the extra pounds I carried from Madonna's cooking. I was a different woman than the last time she saw me back home. But would she notice just how much I'd really changed? Would she notice the darkness in my eyes and how I shoved my shadows within myself?

She had no idea about the blackness living inside me. I'd hid it from her so well.

"Come on, you can sleep on the train. We're going to have a far-out time," I said, grabbing one of her bags. We set off as I grinned with excitement about introducing her to Italy and a mob of cousins and family friends.

"There's a pack of relatives wanting to welcome you. Tomorrow, you'll be their guest of honor for the midday meal. They can't wait to meet you, Grace. You're going to love it."

The next afternoon, Grace and I dodged platters of grilled fish, piles of pasta, and platters of fried zucchini slices and lemon during our family midday dinner. Though Grace was studying Italian, she didn't know the language well. She tried her best to keep up with their chatter. I sat next to her, helping translate and glowing with happiness. I couldn't believe Grace was here.

Grace leaned toward me, saying, "Lenore, this food is *soooo* good here. But I can't eat another bite."

"I know. They eat like this all the time." I sat back in my chair, relaxed. "So eat up because tomorrow we're going with our cousins to their beach club. We'll sail and waterski until your skin turns brown. And wait till you try the cinnamon gelato."

Grace was only experiencing a sunny, carefree Italy and planned to spend the rest of her summer there; I had to teach her about avoiding unwanted attention from Italian guys before I returned home to prepare for attending Davis.

One morning, as we waited for a train to the beach, some teenage boys were horsing around nearby. When they noticed a petite American girl speaking English, they chattered and laughed in Grace's direction, flirting with her.

Innocent and oblivious to their words, Grace smiled at them. Taking advantage of her meager understanding of Italian, their banter suddenly turned raunchy.

Oh, shit! I grabbed Grace's shoulders to turn her attention to me. "Stop! Don't respond to them."

"Why? They're so cute."

"Because they're asking you for blowjobs."

"Are you shitting me?" She scowled in disbelief.

"Who are *you*?" one boy asked me in Italian. "The old maid?"

If I'm an old maid, then so be it. I'd happily let anyone call me that if it meant keeping Grace safe. Ignoring them, I pulled my sister down the platform and away from them. "Do not forget what I'm telling you. Don't attract their attention. It's not like California here."

"Wow, okay. Jeez." She rolled her eyes, but I knew my message had sunk in.

At the end of July, I packed for home.

Standing with Madonna and Grace at the train station, I waited for my train to Rome, wreathed in misery. I couldn't bear to say my goodbye to Madonna. I hated leaving her without knowing if I'd ever see her again.

As my train pulled in, I couldn't stop crying in Madonna's embrace. As she pulled tissues from her purse, I realized she'd never know how much I'd needed her familial affection after leaving Perugia. Because of Madonna, my cough had healed and a bit of my woundedness had subsided.

Leaving Madonna and her serene home by the sea filled me with sadness. But also, I felt deeply relieved to be leaving Italy behind—along with its aggression and trauma. As my train gathered speed, I sat back in my seat, took a few breaths, and shook my head in disbelief. *I'm really going home.* I squirmed with anticipation, eager to return to Mill Valley. Soon, I'd dance right back into my old life with Jackson and our friends, leaving this turbulent year firmly in the past.

Hours later in my taxi to the airport, I watched Rome fade away in the golden afternoon sun, lost in my last glimpses of Italian beauty. Until my driver violently slammed the brakes.

At low speed, we rolled by a nightmarish scene.

On the roadside, a bloodied man lay on the ground as people leaned over him. One man laid his head on the prone man's chest as if listening to his heart.

He looked dead.

This last rearview sight of Italy fit my somber mood. My Italian dream died one night the previous November. Now, eight months later, had this corpse on the roadside symbolized the death of my Italian dream? Was I meant to see this as a reminder that my year abroad was a failure, shrouded with loneliness, trauma, and a constant haze of sadness? I didn't know what the universe was trying to tell me—or if it was trying to tell me anything at all. What I did know for sure was that I couldn't wait to escape into my childhood home and live again with the comfortable and the familiar in the warmth of family.

Two hours later, I slid into my seat on an Air France flight as flight attendants passed complimentary flutes of champagne. I tossed the wine down and asked for another as a giddy happiness flowed inside me.

I could unwind now. I was going home to Mill Valley, Jackson, family, and friends under the shadow of Mount Tamalpais where I was safe and cherished.

18

THE SLEEPING MAIDEN

As we approached San Francisco's airport, we flew right over the peak of Mount Tamalpais, green and recognizable but appearing flat from my perspective above.

That's Mount Tamalpais, the Sleeping Maiden. I'm really home.

I pressed my forehead against the window. As we glided over Mill Valley's village among the redwoods, I choked with emotion.

When I was five, my father asked me, "Can you see her? That's Mount Tamalpais, the Sleeping Maiden."

After crossing the Golden Gate Bridge, we'd emerged from the tunnel above the Sausalito hills. Below, colorful houseboats and white sailboats bobbed on Richardson Bay. Northwest of the bay's mudflats, Mount Tamalpais lay before us.

My eyes had searched for the profile of a sleeping Indian princess silhouetted against the sky on the mountain's ridgeline. I could make out her forehead and nose on the mountain peak. My eyes followed her neckline to her bosom and the rest of her figure slanting down to Mill Valley's round, green hills.

I'd grown up among descendants of Portuguese immigrants, famous authors, bohemian artists, and Marin County's rock royalty, seeking the town's permissive, laid-back culture.

In those days, we kids ran free in the wilds of canyons and forests on foot, bikes, or horses. We scrambled over hillsides dusted with purple lupine and golden California poppies every spring. We splashed in the springs overflowing the creek beds and chased each other through lush swaths of poison oak. Our moms had no idea of our whereabouts. Always, Mount Tamalpais watched over us. At dinnertime, we burst through our front doors, dirty and itchy, stomachs growling yet brimming with joy.

As teenagers, Jackson and I rambled her trails, named Hoo-Koo-E-Koo, Hogback, or Bootjack, crossing cool meadows scented with wild fennel and walking in and out of cloud and fog. Alongside a tumbling creek and waterfalls, we hiked down the Steep Ravine Trail leafy with wild ferns and miner's lettuce, which opened upon sun-washed grasslands. We traipsed through cool redwood groves and hot, dry slopes of yerba santa and manzanita. The older boys who invented mountain biking whizzed past us, burning out brakes or breaking bones.

Sometimes, Jackson and I lay in the tall grass on Bolinas Ridge over-looking a flashing sea as vast as our futures. There, I dreamed of becoming a writer. Later, I'd fill journal pages about Mount Tamalpais and its sage-scented upper trails, November's abundant mushrooms, and the jaw-dropping views of Mill Valley, Angel Island, and San Francisco beyond, all sparkling in the Western light.

The mountain sheltered me from Pacific storms slamming into its slopes and the heavy rains draining into its valleys. Her watershed filled our creeks and abundant springs and nurtured coastal redwoods hundreds of years old.

The Sleeping Maiden became the verdant landscape of my child-hood, lying peacefully as the Pacific's fog blanketed her against the night.

She was always there when, as a Catholic schoolgirl, I stared out my classroom window, a dreamer watching the afternoon mists waft over her ridges. She was there when I climbed Kite Hill and decided to travel the world after high school graduation at seventeen.

Now, sitting back into my airline seat on my return home, I was eager to escape into the serenity of the wild mountain, roam her trails with Jackson, and find shelter and peace once again.

Throughout my life, Dad had sheltered me too, like Mount Tamalpais.

I couldn't wait to take refuge in his house. I looked forward to being surrounded by my family, but I wondered if they'd notice my sad eyes or see how I'd changed. And I wondered what I should say if they did. I'd lived so long traumatized and mute, alone in a distant country. Although time creates distance, it cannot erase trauma. I feared I'd never be able to say aloud what happened to me. Not even now in the safety of Mill Valley.

I shuddered inside with a flicker of unease. *Maybe I, too, am a sleeping maiden.*

Would I allow myself to become cloaked in the comforting haze of Pacific fogs and stubbornly cling to my old life even though so much had changed? Behind my shield of denial, I remained exposed—vulnerable to a truth I refused to confront. Would I be forced to recognize the young woman I'd become, or would I ignore the loss of my innocence in hopes of being shielded from my pain?

19

COMING HOME

After an early morning landing, I swept through the double doors of customs when a strange boy grabbed me and hugged my waist.

Entangled in jetlag's blur, I stared at him, not recognizing my youngest brother. At ten years old, he had transformed in a year, several inches taller, his hair and eyebrows bleached blond after hours in the pool with his swim team. Beyond him, my family—Mom, Dad, and my other two brothers—smiled through tears, eager for my hug. Everyone looked different yet the same.

I fell into their arms.

Home.

My family's faces, like Grace's when we reunited in Rome, revealed how different I looked. I told myself the changes weren't a big deal—not the short hair, not the added weight, and not the burden of trauma I now carried. No one held a knife to my throat then, nor did they now. I hadn't died—what happened was over, and I lived to talk about it. Except I wouldn't say a word.

Stepping into my home felt exhilarating. The air felt the same. Everything looked the same. And I was the same. I had to tell myself this to start believing it.

Friends—girls who had known me my entire life—dropped by. During our joyous reunion, we plopped onto the living room carpet to catch up. I concentrated on our chatter as we picked up the threads of our lives, sharing news of break-ups, new boyfriends, and even a marriage. I shifted on the carpet, noticing the same expressions my family wore at the airport. My friends saw a physical difference in me too. But only I knew the truth about why I must have looked so uncomfortable in my skin.

After their short visit, my friends left, and I was overcome by jetlag. I studied myself in the bathroom mirror, focusing on my sad eyes and serious face, on the pain that lay beneath the surface. I took a shower and a long nap, hoping to calm my anxiety. When I woke up, I felt refreshed and ready to see Jackson.

Jackson knew I'd be over at his house as soon as possible after my arrival. But getting behind the wheel after one year meant I had to figure out how to drive again. And not like an Italian.

Driving to Sausalito, I caught a reflection of my round face in the rearview mirror and gulped. He would notice how different I looked too.

Before I left for Perugia, we plotted Jackson's summer visit to Italy. Then, after our letters had grown so infrequent, plans never materialized. Now, adults at twenty, we would either pick up where we left off or acknowledge the distance that had grown between us and go our separate ways.

Buzzing with excitement, hoping for the former, I bounced up to the entry to step inside Jackson's home overlooking the bay and its sailboats.

His mom, ever gracious, said, "Lenore, welcome back."

Smiling, I said, "Oh, thank you. I've missed you all."

As part of his bohemian family for over two and a half years before Italy, I had reveled in the fun atmosphere there as Jackson played the grand piano and his siblings and friends paraded in and out.

I turned around looking for Jackson to see him grinning at me; he hadn't changed a bit. And he didn't seem to notice how different I looked.

Jackson saw only me.

He saw only me though I dressed like an Italian girl in tight jeans, a white shirt, and a well-cut jacket. To set off my green eyes, I wore heavy kohl eyeliner, fashionable in Italy but considered slutty in Marin.

When he encircled me in a long hug, I eagerly held his familiar body tight. Then, I sighed, failing to sense my old, passionate hunger for him. When we broke apart, I couldn't look into his eyes. Instead, I looked at my feet.

Sitting down together, we kept a comfortable distance whereas, at one time, we couldn't keep our hands off each other. As we chatted about his Berkeley life and my Davis plans, I felt a sinking sensation in my chest. The tether to my former life with him had frayed, slipping from my grasp.

I searched his handsome face for my answer. His eyes, his smile—everything—was the same. And yet, I felt nothing. A year apart had extinguished what we once had, and now, with seventy miles between our universities, I realized we were no longer us.

I couldn't connect with the girl I had been before Italy. That girl was fearless, madly in love, up for anything. The girl I was now felt numb and hollow. Could I ever become her again?

"Sorry I didn't write enough," said Jackson as we sank into the couch in the living room. "School was so busy."

"Well, I didn't write much either," I replied, my voice steady but distant.

"So, you had lots of adventures in Italy?"

"Oh, so many," I said with a smile that felt practiced. "Spring break in Greece was amazing. What about you? Where are you living next year?"

"I'm moving into an apartment on Ashby with some guys. They're pretty cool. You?"

"Grace and I are moving into an off-campus dorm. It even has a pool," I said, trying to sound enthusiastic. "Have you decided on your major?"

"Yeah, math and French."

"Double major. Impressive. I'm still figuring mine out. Davis doesn't have a journalism program, so I'm not sure yet."

"Yeah," Jackson said.

A long pause grew between us. With nothing left to say, we stepped outside, under the purple wisteria where we had first met.

Jackson pulled me into a final embrace, and I clung to the moment, knowing it was our last.

"Well, I'll see you later," I said softly.

"Yeah, see you later," he replied.

As I stepped away from him, the weight of leaving not only Jackson but also the girl I once was sank in. A wave of sorrow struck me. *How can I move forward without him when he was so important to me for so long? If we break up, does it mean I am incapable of love?*

Yet I walked away, knowing there was no going back. When I got into the car, my shoulders dropped. We had been so close, always thrilled to be together. Now, we'd never be together again. This pain felt different from what I'd lived with, yet it was a necessary pain. My chest ached, and I looked at my sad eyes in the rearview. Maybe I wasn't so numb after all.

I shivered. Why did I think I could fly home and land lightly into my old life?

I rubbed my eyes, exhausted from jetlag and too much change.

Okay, you can't live in the rearview mirror. I started up the engine, pressed the accelerator, and drove home.

20

SHADOWED AND HUNTED DOWN

Jane Fonda pushed her long hair off her pretty face and tilted it toward the sun as she sighed. She was so beautiful.

In the shady quad of University of California, Davis, the Hollywood actress and activist spoke to a noontime crowd during her husband's primary campaign for US Senator.

After two years at the College of Marin and a year abroad, I thought settling back into American college life would be easy. However, amid classes, dorm parties, and late-night library sessions, I confronted culture shock. In confusion, I grappled with my new circumstances by freaking out at the strangest moments.

Instead of attending classical music concerts in a Renaissance-era venue, I got splattered with beer at keg parties. Instead of sipping espresso with sophisticated Italian girls, frat guys shoved me around during $1 burger nights. Instead of dining on tender strands of pasta, I valiantly shoveled down bland, processed dorm food from the eighth ring of hell. As students blasted rock music from their dorm rooms, I didn't recognize a single song. And when they passed around a joint, I panicked.

I'd been away too long.

Around my dorm, I drew curiosity from everyone once they learned I spoke fluent Italian after a year abroad.

"Oh, say something in Italian!" they'd say.

After the one-hundredth time, I lost my patience and replied in melodic Italian, "What the fuck do you want me to say, shithead?"

"Oooh," they'd croon. "That sounds so beautiful."

As I began my UC Davis adventure, I knew darkness had followed me, and the ghost of the girl I was in Italy haunted me. Amid the partying, I stood silent and alone, holding a beer, shifting from foot to foot, not fitting in anywhere or with anyone. Stuck in two worlds, I felt neither American nor Italian. Everyone eased into campus life, but I'd missed the memo. Isolated, I had trouble making friends, and I filled my journal with an overwhelming loneliness.

Around campus, flyers from the student health center offered help, yet counseling never entered my mind. Imprisoned by guilt and shame for allowing myself to be sexually assaulted, I held to the belief that the rape had been "no big deal." And that's why that ghost of the girl had taken up residence inside me, knocking at my conscience, demanding I give her attention.

That winter, Grace and I went to a New Year's Eve party at the University of San Francisco.

After midnight, we left the festivities to eat at one of the City's finest eateries, the International House of Pancakes, on Lombard Street.

After stumbling into the packed entrance, we sat on vinyl banquettes next to the hostess to await a table. Two older guys came in and plopped down next to us.

"Where you girls from?" slurred one, his breath reeking of stale cigarettes and alcohol.

"Mill Valley," I said.

"Oh, Marin girls! In the City for some slumming?" said the other over the restaurant racket. He leaned in too closely, his greasy jeans threatening to rub against my leg. Creeped out, I twisted myself toward Grace to ensure she hadn't caught his trash talk.

The first guy stood up and reached into his pocket for a cigarette. Weaving above me, he tried to light one as his long, dirty hair hung near his flaming match.

I bristled inside when he sat next to Grace and mumbled about the horrible things he was "gonna do" to her sexually. My skin crawled.

"Grace, move away from that guy," I said hoarsely, tugging her arm and bringing her closer to me.

"Huh, what?" she said, drunk and enjoying her night. My sister stood barely five feet tall and weighed a hundred pounds wet.

Panic bristled up my back as the beer and marijuana from the party clouded my thinking. We *had* to get away from these fuckers.

"Ready to be seated?" asked the hostess.

I jumped up, saying, "Oh, yes," grateful to her for pulling us away from these assholes.

Sitting in our booth as fear gnawed my stomach, I said, "Hey. Those guys, they were threatening you. We gotta watch out for them."

"No, they weren't," Grace said, slurring her answer.

Naïve and innocent, she didn't take me seriously. Grace wasn't equipped to spot danger like I was.

I pressed on. "No, really. They were threatening us, Grace. They could follow us out of the restaurant."

"They're just high," she said as if I were overreacting.

Twisting around, I searched for those guys among the crowded tables but never found them. After our orders arrived, Grace downed chocolate chip pancakes as I stared at my uneaten plate, fears circling in my mind. *They're going to wait for us outside. I just know it. They're going to try something.*

It took an eternity to pay the check and rush out the door. In the parking lot, stiff with fright, I moved as if wading in mud toward our car. I needed to escape, but I was afraid to go too fast in case I would run us right into danger. I hated not knowing where those scummy guys were.

I shoved my key into the door lock, saying, "Get in. And lock your door."

Finally, we rolled onto Lombard Street, my hands squeezing the steering wheel.

Grace passed out before we reached the Golden Gate Bridge; my

During my 21st birthday party, I struggled to hide my shadows.
Image courtesy of the author's collection.

anxious breathing wouldn't calm until we crossed into Marin.

Old anxiety and fear had shadowed me from Italy and hunted me down at home.

Would I forever scan crowds with unease, keeping a constant watch, avoiding dim places, and seeing every man walking toward me as a potential attacker?

Devastation overtook me—not a good thing for a young woman searching for herself and her place in the world.

Back on the UC Davis campus, a lonely Saturday lay before me—an entire free day on a rare sunny January afternoon. I headed downstairs to join the crowd gathered around our pool. Yes, our off-campus dorm had a pool; people called our dorm the rich kids' dorm.

I sat on a lounge chair for a moment when restlessness clenched my guts.

Music blasted, beer cans popped, and guys yelled from their third-floor balcony.

I had heard that my college days would be the best time of my life. I felt cheated. I had to get out of there. I had thought living in an American dorm would be a dream—the camaraderie, the pranks, the parties. But now, living among two hundred people, I cursed under my breath amid the constant racket, noisy steak nights, loud TV football games, and all the stomping up and down the stairways.

I felt powerful walking toward the bike racks, escaping the crowd to hop on my bike and pedal onto the quiet street.

I rode straight out of town, entering a world of peacefulness in expansive nature on empty two-lane country roads. I rolled into the countryside, past farmer fields redolent of alfalfa where a good silence reigned and God felt nearby. Crows cried above the broad squares of farmland in the flat, pure light. I found solace in the Central Valley's ordered fields where the farmers had planted in straight, organized rows, fruit trees blossomed in spring, and rice fields turned orange in August. I stopped my bike, placed my foot on the rough asphalt, and, breathing hard, watched the clouds in the blue sky above.

I absorbed the dead quiet. And I needed the quiet. I paused to listen to the wind's rustle and feel the sun upon my skin. Space expanded, and everything felt soft, soothing, and welcoming with no people around me for miles. Finally, I felt in control. My mind could only take so much noise, so many people, and so much pressure to study hard for good grades.

Enjoying my solitude, I pedaled on, following roads that offered more escape routes. Once I felt restored after flying around the countryside, I turned my bike around to head back to my dorm.

After dinner, I went to my room, where I usually spent my Saturday nights alone. Shoving corn chips into my mouth, I scowled at my unsuccessful social life yet had no idea how to fix it. As I heard parties starting up, I wondered why nobody ever invited me to their parties or why guys never asked me out.

Brushing away crumbs, I shoved myself off my bed and walked up one floor to visit Grace's dorm room. A freshman sprung free at nineteen, my sister caroused and joked with roommates and random boys, a can of beer in her hand.

Sadness ran through me; Grace always looked comfortable around guys as she reveled in endless parties. And many guys liked her, paying attention to her or winding up in her room for an after-party.

Surrounded by strangers, I felt sapped of the energy to get social and join the college monkey business. What was wrong with me? I retreated to my bed, feeling lonely, friendless, and doomed.

21

THE GHOST AND
THE PRANKSTER

By spring, the college town of Davis slowly grew on me with its simple
Central Valley small-town vibe. I bicycled through streets shaded by
immense trees where our professors lived in older, stately homes. In the
sleepy downtown, I watched local children ride their bikes to the ice cream
shop. Or I'd catch a movie at the lone theatre.

On warm valley evenings, I studied next to an open window in the
library, listening on earphones to the "La Primavera" concerto from Vivaldi's
Four Seasons. I started writing for the campus newspaper, reviewing art and
cultural events. I went spring skiing with new friends. When a dorm-wide
water fight erupted, I jumped in, laughing so hard it hurt. During a keg
party, Grace and I downed brews atop a red double-decker bus swaying
around town.

I finally seemed to enjoy settling into collegiate life.

In the spring, I met a guy.

I noticed him during an impromptu barbecue in a park with some dormmates. Tanned and shirtless, he wore an entire six-pack of beer, cans of Bud tucked carefully into every pocket of his white overalls. Brown-eyed and curly-haired, he reminded me of the Italian boys of Perugia though he severely lacked in the fashion department.

His name was Rob.

As students passed paper plates of burgers, buns, and fixings, Rob offered me garlic bread, saying, "Here, have some."

Smelling the grilled bread's intoxicating aroma, I took a generous bite as he watched. A sudden pain blasted its way throughout my mouth.

Holy shit, somebody doesn't know how to make garlic bread.

Spitting and coughing, I examined my slice, which was thickly smeared with raw garlic and butter.

"Who made this?"

"Arnie," he answered innocently, pointing to a guy who grew up in Chinatown.

Without guilt, he happily imposed the garlic bread on more unsuspecting diners. Despite his prank, I joined Rob, his roommate, and another girl for an all-nighter in their dorm room, drinking and playing a French card game, Mille Bornes.

It was so nice to jump into something spontaneous and fun. We bounced on two waterbeds, playing and laughing and talking and smoking dope and drinking more beer until we collapsed.

When the smell of bacon wafted in from our cafeteria, a groggy voice said we should eat. Lying atop a waterbed, wearing my clothes from yesterday's party, I knew I risked a walk of shame without any reason for the shame. I turned over and opened my eyes in front of Rob's face; he kissed me in the light of the rising sun.

From that day on, I found him outside the cafeteria every night, waiting for me before dinner. He held doors open for me. He offered me rides back to our dorm after my class. He appeared at my side at random dorm parties. And I began hanging out in his room, getting to know him and his roommate better.

One night, at a party in a student apartment, he revealed more of his wicked, sly sense of humor, this time with dog food.

He grabbed a handful of dog biscuits he found in the kitchen, embellished them with yellow spray cheese, and nestled them among olives, cheese, and pickles on our hostess's hors d'oeuvres plate.

He held his finger to his lips. "Don't say a thing."

We sat back on a couch together with deadpan expressions to watch hilarity ensue.

"How can you be so funny?" I asked after the partyers figured out the ruse. "You're an engineering major. You're supposed to be dull and boring."

"Nope. And I'm not only funny, but I can fix anything. Anything. Because engineering isn't work to me—it's fun." He leaned into me. "And I'm going to be an excellent engineer."

Inseparable after two weeks, we attended keg parties and crowded bars, where he'd find me a seat and introduce me around. When I went to movies, ballets, and art shows to review for the campus newspaper, he joined me and enjoyed it. I smiled at his respect for women and impeccable manners, perhaps learned at his Jesuit boys-only high school, perhaps at home.

And I appreciated how Rob conjured great, spontaneous ideas for our adventures.

"Let's cut class tomorrow and go skiing," he'd say before skillfully attaching ski racks to his used Toyota. "Student tickets at Sugar Bowl on Tuesdays are five bucks."

On a ski slope, Rob, a robust and graceful skier, frowned when I froze, stiffened with dread atop a black diamond trail.

"It's way too steep."

"Come on, Lenore. Show some balls."

I tilted my head. "Rob, I don't have any balls. I'm a woman."

That took a moment to sink in. "Well, then, follow me. I'll go slow."

Skiing behind him, I allowed all fear to drop away.

Rob raced past me as I bombed down my second black diamond run. He turned around and faced me, skiing backward.

"You're going too slow."

I laughed and slid down a steep slope of falling hard for him.

Running around with my favorite trickster, I kept our blossoming relationship private. Then, when we got super serious, I couldn't keep it from Grace any longer.

One afternoon, I entered her dorm room and found her on her bed as she painted the pages in her textbook in yellow marker.

"Hey, I just wanted you to know I'm going away for the weekend," I told her. "With Rob. To his family's cabin at Tahoe."

She shoved her book aside and sat up in bed. "Okay, what's going on?"

I let out a big breath—time to go public. "Well, I'm crazy about him. He's just so nice. He even holds doors open for me. Who does that nowadays? Yeah, he's cute. And funny. But I don't know him that well, you know?"

"Yeah, but you will."

Rob and I raced to Lake Tahoe for an intimate weekend. As we snuggled in front of the fire, Rob wrapped me into a big hug, sheltering me from a cold world as a warm sense of security ran through me.

We crawled into bed together for the first time. As Rob touched me, surprising pain and resistance unfurled inside me.

"Stop, stop, stop!" I pushed him away.

"What's wrong?"

An old abyss of devastation cracked open, and I fell in. His touch reminded me of Gul touching me the same way. I hadn't been intimate with anyone since then. Feeling raw, confused, and shocked at my reaction, I struggled to find my words. I paused, gathered myself, and said, "I have to tell you something."

I wasn't sure why I felt comfortable sharing my secret with him, but for the first time, my mouth formed the words to voice my painful history. As Rob listened to me in the mountain darkness, his face slowly hardened.

When my words stopped, he pulled me close, saying, "That makes me so angry that I want to do that guy in. No one deserves that. Especially someone as tender and sweet as you. I'll never let anything happen to you again."

Rob took a long time to fall asleep, but he held me in his arms all night.

Having finally released my words into the light of his devotion, I felt the power of what had happened in Italy diminish, and I fell into a peaceful sleep.

After earning my trust, Rob cared for me at my worst. Especially on the night he and his buddies threw a fancy booze and cigar party. I joined in, dressed in my most elegant dress as Rob held his lighter to my first cigar.

Later, after smoking two cigars down to the nibs and drinking too many Singapore Slings, I locked myself in a bathroom, weaved over the toilet, and splattered my dress with vomit. I banned Rob from entering as he knocked at the door.

"Let me help you."

I hated the thought of him seeing me like this, so I yelled, "Noooo, don't come in."

"I'll hold your forehead for you."

I cracked the door open, banging his foot. I was teary from retching, and mascara ran down my cheeks. "I'm sorry. I'm so fucked up."

"No, you're fine. Let me help clean your gown."

Gown? Who says "gown" these days? Rob's words struck me as refined and classy. He was a classy guy. That was the last thing I remembered before passing out in his bed.

In the morning, Rob's smile warmed the pounding pain in my head. Wincing from his own hangover, he got me pain relievers and water.

Had I ever imagined feeling so safe and warm? As my shelter from the storm, Rob's ardor gave me hope that my painful past would never resurface to dim my life with loneliness and depression as it had during my California re-entry.

Being with Rob felt like I'd traveled on the right path—a path toward happiness and healing. In a short time, I got to know him well. I *knew* him. We had a lot in common: Italian blood, growing up in large families (Rob was the middle kid of seven), and attending Catholic schools until college.

Over the months, our romance grew torrid. One evening, as we studied for exams before Christmas break, I said, "I've got to tell you something. My advisor said that I have enough credits to graduate early."

"How come? I thought you were only a junior."

"Remember when I challenged all those Italian exams? Walked in and just took them? Well, I passed them all, and now I've got enough credits to graduate next June."

"Oh," he said, tapping his pen hard on a notebook.

"So, I guess I'll go home and get a job in the City. A writing job, I'm hoping."

"Well, great." Displeasure raced across his face; he had another year to go.

On New Year's Eve, Rob invited me to his hometown of San Jose for a party thrown by high school buddies. He drove through the flats of the vast city for what seemed an hour.

He parked at a house where a loud party bled into the night. We

Smooth sailing on the Bay with my new boyfriend, Rob.
Image courtesy of the author's collection.

joined the drunken revels inside, who were mostly guys from his boys-only high school, all friendly, welcoming, and very loaded. I watched Rob join their camaraderie, hugging, back-slapping, and laughing amid the repeated greeting, "Hey man, good to see you!"

Trying to avoid beer splashing on my jeans, I stood next to him, seeing another side of him as I listened to their banter about their illustrious football team and state championships.

At midnight, he slurred his words as we toasted the new year. Suddenly, he pulled me into a bathroom and said, "Come here, come here."

"Wait. I don't have to go," I said.

He closed the toilet lid and sat me down. Swaying above me, he asked, "Will you marry me?"

Despite his bizarre location for a marriage proposal, and my intoxicated state, I ecstatically said yes. I may have been hammered, but I had no doubts about my protector, my sweetheart, the man who made me laugh.

The next morning, I awoke in his parents' house, gripped with worry. *Did he really propose to me? Or am I a victim of another prank?* With an unbearable intensity, I stared at him over coffee, sitting hungover in his family's kitchen.

"Do you remember what you asked me last night?"

He grinned. "Oh, yes."

"But wait. Who proposes to someone sitting on a toilet?"

He stood and embraced me, saying, "I can't help it. I love you so much. You are mine forever. And I adore your nose. It's so cute."

We kept our engagement a secret for a year, a thrilling reality, ours alone. After surviving Italy, I quickly settled into my new life with Rob, savoring the luxury of loving a man I trusted. His constant passion made me feel secure and safe. The cold ghost of the girl I used to be, the one haunted by shadows of the past, had retreated; I hoped for good. I had no fear about marrying him so young—I knew in my bones we were meant for each other.

I was on a path to marry a descendant of a Perugino—that's why Rob's looks had first reminded me of the boys in Perugia. His great-grandparents, tomato farmers named Marianelli, had emigrated to San Jose after the death of an infant girl. This tragedy perhaps spurred their courage to abandon Italy and begin anew, growing tomatoes in the fertile Santa Clara Valley.

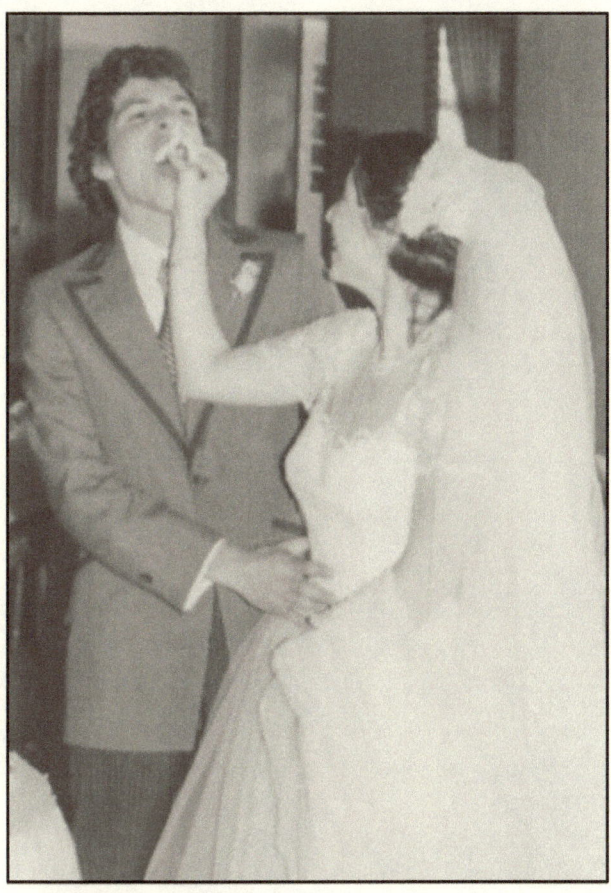

Looking dainty in Mom's 1950s wedding gown as I shoved cake into Rob's mouth.
Image courtesy of the author's collection.

After Rob's college graduation, we celebrated our bond with a big Italian wedding, surrounded by family and friends, all two hundred and seventy-five of them.

Our life together suddenly traveled at the speed of light, as if we knew our near future demanded we rush into the next stage of our adult lives. Right after we married, we bought a house. A year and a half later, overflowing with bliss, we welcomed our daughter, Claire.

22

DRESSED UP FOR A CATASTROPHE

One morning, as I nursed seven-month-old Claire in our bed, I watched with sleepy eyes as my husband got ready for work at a Kaiser Aluminum plant as the company's youngest plant engineer.

Stepping out of the shower, Rob said, "Honey, I think there's something wrong. There's, like, a vein or something on my testicle. Remember how I noticed it a couple of months ago? Now it's gotten bigger."

"Well, call the doctor. Get it checked out. It's probably nothing."

"Maybe it's from having too much sex," he said, laughing and kissing Claire's forehead and then mine.

Later that morning, I was thrilled about my first outing as a new mom, attending a relative's charity lunch and fashion show at the Fairmont Hotel. I bundled Claire into my car and drove to Mill Valley so Mom could babysit.

After placing Claire into her joyful grandmother's arms, I headed into my childhood bathroom to change. Trembling with excitement, I dabbed on make-up and changed into a new blue silk dress and high heels. Twisting my hair around a curling iron, I smiled at the mirror.

I can do this. I can manage a new baby and enjoy some glamour in my life.

Mom broke my reverie by pounding on the bathroom door. "Lenore, you have to come out!"

She could be so dramatic.

"Rob just called. He has cancer!"

I opened the door and found her cradling Claire.

"He has to have emergency surgery tomorrow morning," she said, her eyes steely. "You've got to meet him at the hospital right now. I'll take care of Claire. Go. Now."

Dazed, I gathered my things and got into my car, all dressed up for a catastrophe in my new silk dress and heels. The City on the bay looked bright, spotlit by the sun poking through the fog above the Berkeley hills. What a beautiful December day—clear and splashed with sunshine—a gorgeous day that mocked me. Time telescoped as I raced to the hospital.

Too many thoughts ricocheted inside my head as my fingers gripped the steering wheel, working hard to keep terror at bay. Tears brimmed as I thought about my poor Rob, the center of my life, alone in a hospital bed. I blinked them back.

I found Rob wearing a gown, looking tan and healthy but pale from shock.

"The doctor says it's 90 percent that it's cancer. So, they're going to remove my testicle tomorrow morning and biopsy it. Then, they'll know more."

My arms flew to him, and we held each other, silent and numb until more words came.

"Lenore, you have to tell my parents."

"Okay," I whispered. I put it off until a stinky dinner tray arrived, which Rob ignored since fear had stripped him of his appetite.

Outside, the sky had darkened.

"Lenore, you better go make that call."

My stomach sank. *I hate this, destroying his parents with one call.* I felt absurd in my fancy dress, my heels clicking down empty hospital hallways as I searched for a phone.

I'd die if someone told me Claire had cancer and needed emergency surgery.

Agony overtook me, and my head spun. Then a quick, fierce reality sank in. *Oh my God, Claire could lose her dad. What's going to happen to us?*

Going through the motions like a robot, I dialed my in-laws at a pay phone. My mother-in-law cheerfully answered and asked how the baby was doing. Living her old life, she had no idea I'd called to jettison her into a terrifying one.

I spoke slow, somber words. "I have some news. For both of you. We're at the hospital because they found a tumor on Rob's testicle. There's a 90 percent chance that it's cancer." I paused.

Silence.

"Tomorrow morning, he has emergency surgery to remove it. We'll know more after the biopsy comes back in three to six days."

More silence.

Then, Rob's mom asked, "Where's the baby?"

"She's with my mom."

"Okay, honey. Well, let us know what happens tomorrow," she said. "We'll go to eight o'clock Mass tomorrow to pray for him. Please tell Rob that we love him."

Afterward, I drifted, lost, through vacant corridors, trying to find Rob's room. I swallowed my tears with an automatic swiftness, an expert at shutting out trauma.

At ten the next morning, clad in blue scrubs, Rob's surgeon, Dr. Abad, emerged from Recovery through double doors, doors I'd stared at for hours, awaiting his news.

"Come with me," he said brusquely. He led me down a hall painted an unoffensive green, opened a door, and ushered me into a room large enough for two chairs.

I screamed inside my head. *What a charade. Putting me in a private room for a quiet conversation. What bullshit.*

We took our seats underneath a buzzing blue, fluorescent light.

"You have to be strong. It's cancer."

My head felt as if it swooped down to the floor and back up again.

"So, I expect his testicle to be malignant," he said. "Testicular cancer is a disease of young men and has an unknown survival rate."

No, we're too young for this!

More words came: "Embryonal cell carcinoma."

Stunned, I rubbed my palms on the chair's rigid wooden arms, working hard to concentrate on words I never should've had to hear. More words came, words that bashed inside my skull.

"A second surgery . . . chemo . . . sterility."

No, you don't understand. He's only twenty-four years old!

Then, Dr. Abad tossed his harshest words yet into the suffocating room. "You may want to get pregnant right now. Before his second surgery. After we remove the lymph nodes, he'll be sterile."

I blinked rapidly, not absorbing anything. "What? Wait," I stammered. "We have a seven-month-old baby. I'm breastfeeding her—how can I get pregnant?"

He stood up, signaling the end of our meeting. "One step at a time, okay? You can go see him in Recovery now."

Fighting an avalanche of tears, I stumbled into Recovery and found Rob unconscious underneath piles of blankets.

A nurse rolled a stool over to his bed for me. I stared at his handsome face as it dissolved into a blur through my tears. I rocked unconsciously, engulfed by fear. Watching him breathe, I shook my head in disbelief. Damn it! Yesterday, life was so simple. He went to the doctor to get checked out. Just in case. Something on a testicle. I'd thought nothing of it.

Oh my God. Rob might die. And Claire and I will be alone. This was supposed to be a time of beginnings, not endings.

I straightened up on my stool. I had to focus. I had to make sure I was strong for Rob and that he saw my strength when he woke up. Dabbing tears with his sheet, I held his hand as he drifted out of unconsciousness and his eyes opened.

In an unfamiliar voice, he mumbled, "There's my best girl."

Rob placed his bag on our bed after I brought him home from the hospital. "So we're going to try for another baby?" he asked.

I sat on our bed. "Well, by my calculations, we've only got three weeks before your second surgery, so no promises."

"Can you even get pregnant while breastfeeding?" he asked as he undressed.

"It's possible. So, if God wants us to have another baby, we will."

"But we won't know if you're pregnant until after my surgery, right? And I'll already be . . ." he said. He sank into our bed with a slight groan.

"Yeah. By then you'll be sterile, so this is our last chance," I said.

"Maybe we should freeze some sperm."

"I already checked. Do you know where the nearest sperm bank is? In Los Angeles. We don't have the time or the money to go down there."

Rob lay back on his pillow, rubbing his face from worry, and said,

"You know, you might be a widow with two little kids instead of one."

I felt old and worn at twenty-five. My fingers twisted the edge of the bedsheet. Why did we have to make such a big decision? Why couldn't our life go back to normal? I couldn't take this. Seeking comfort, I snuggled up to him and said, "My mom will be here soon with the baby."

Rob let out a big breath. "I can't wait to see her and hold her."

He sat up on one elbow. "Look, let's just take this a day at a time, okay? If we get pregnant, great. If not, that'll be okay, too. But I would like a son."

I smiled. "I'll do my best."

The phone rang. Dad was calling from his office: "I got Rob in for a second opinion with the top testicular cancer guy over at Stanford. His office will call you to set things up. Okay, I got to call somebody else now." He hung up.

Minutes later, he called back. "I got Rob a consultation with a radiologist friend in the City. He'll review his case and give us his opinion on chemo versus radiation."

"Wonderful. Everything helps, Dad. Thanks!"

"You're welcome, Lenore. You doing okay? Need anything?"

"No, not right now. Just praying a lot."

"Yeah, that will help."

Dad was still my warrior chieftain who tried to protect me from everything. I hung up, feeling the light of his love.

During Rob's second surgery, I paged through random magazines in the waiting room. I came across a quote: "Being deeply loved by someone gives you strength while loving someone deeply gives you courage." The author attributed was Lao Tzu though I doubted whether he was actually responsible for these words.

It didn't matter who'd first uttered them. I stopped and re-read them, absorbing their truth. Did I have the courage to dedicate my life to nurturing Rob even if he might be leaving us? Even at my most vulnerable with two babies?

I had no answer.

For four years, Rob had surrounded me with his ardor as I danced into a new realm of health, joy, and bliss, losing the extra weight I'd gained while in Italy and growing my hair longer.

I thought I had matured a lot after my traumatic time in Italy. However, since I had told Rob about that one night, any time I brought it up, he looked at me with pain in his eyes and said, "Please, I don't want to hear about it."

If merely talking about it hurt him so much, how much more had it hurt me? On my own, I dealt with my traumatic memories by shoving them beneath the surface. I treasured Rob so much I hated to see him hurt, so I locked my ordeal away to concentrate on our marriage and baby.

And now this? An immense fear of the future grabbed me and held on. Dread became my constant companion. Whether in the grocery store or changing a diaper, I could never escape it.

In our gray world, our future happiness depended on a second surgery and a single test, a biopsy of his lymph nodes.

On the night after his surgery, I told family members gathered at our home what the surgeon said and how Rob got through everything okay. Then, Dad walked through my front door, wearing his suit from work.

He kissed me and said, "Just saw Rob in the ICU." His white, grief-stricken face told me he cared for Rob as much as he cared for his own sons. "Got any Scotch?"

I'd never seen Dad drink, except at parties. But on that night, I watched a sad scene: my silent father filling a tall water glass with Scotch and drinking it down to ease his pain.

Despite his suffering, Dad tried to shelter us from this trauma by giving us hope with expert doctors and second opinions. He became my anchor, and it calmed me to know he had our backs.

One morning, a pale sun poured into the window of Rob's hospital room, where he had to recover for two weeks after his second surgery. For the first five days, we awaited his biopsy results; his testicle biopsy had already come back positive. Half-awake, Rob lay in bed, holding my hand as I read a spiritual book, *When Bad Things Happen to Good People*, by a great Jewish rabbi.

Rob's surgeon strode into the room, held his hands up wide, and declared, "Your lymph nodes are clear, Mr. Greiner."

"Ah, that's great news," said Rob in a weak voice.

I jumped up to gently hold him as we laughed and cried.

The doctor sat down in a chair, holding some papers. "So, in this case, we caught it in stage one. And if you catch it in time, you're 90 percent cured."

"Thank you!" I said.

"Wow, that's amazing," said Rob.

"Okay, so you get better, and we'll get you out of here in a few days. We'll see you again at your next checkup." Then he was gone.

23

ANOTHER TERRITORY, DARK AND UNMAPPED

After the oncologist left, I looked at a grinning Rob. "I have something to tell you even better than that."

"What? What could be better than that?"

I leaned close to his face and said, "I'm pregnant. I think you're going to get your son."

Rob placed his hand on my flat stomach. "I can't believe it. Really? Are you sure?"

"My doctor said my test was positive. I almost kissed her," I said, smiling in disbelief that our luck had turned so completely around after six weeks of hell.

Eight months later, we welcomed a tiny, dark-haired bundle with Rob's eyes. Little Hunter made our family complete. Loving and caring for my two babies, I took things one day at a time as a grateful mother and wife. Rob grew strong enough to go back to work, taking off in his pickup every morning.

One evening at dinnertime, I turned the blender off and poured Rob's liquified chicken into a bowl of hot broth for his meal.

"You know, this has been going on too long, Rob. It's not normal to keep blending your food so you can eat," I said, feeling like a nagging wife. "And you've lost more weight." Concerned, I encouraged him to eat whenever I could.

"I know. I know. I just can't swallow well. The food gets stuck."

One of the seven signs of cancer.

"You have to call your doctor."

We looked at each other in terror. Rob slumped in his chair. "Okay, I'll call him."

Cancer is a formidable foe. When Hunter turned seven months old, our second nightmare began. Rob's cancer had returned.

A few days later, Rob walked in from work, where he'd spoken with his doctor about his scan results on the phone. As soon as I saw his face, he didn't need to say a word. We both *knew*.

He got himself a beer and sat at the kitchen table stiffly. With *Mister Roger's Neighborhood* theme song playing in the background, I learned about an ominous mass growing behind his heart, pressing on his aorta.

"It's as big as my fist," he said. "I need to see an oncologist about chemotherapy."

There it was. That word. *Chemotherapy.*

"So it's malignant?"

"Yeah. The cancer has spread."

We sat in silence.

"How could this happen?" I asked, rubbing my face. "Over a year ago, they said you were 90 percent cured."

I stood up and paced. "You know," I said, "these fucking doctors don't know anything, and now—" I stopped myself from saying Rob was going to die.

Looking defeated, Rob sighed and said, "I don't know." Then, "Oh, almost forgot. You've got to take my scans to that radiologist in the City for a second opinion."

I felt grateful for a task, something to do. I had too much time to think, my thoughts hardening and haunting me incessantly. I couldn't function, and I couldn't take care of the kids or Rob. So I wore a blank face and carried on.

I drove into the City the following day to deliver Rob's scans. Extremely overtired, I pondered this worthless time spent on doctors. And for what? On the freeway, I yelled in my car, "Fuck you, you fucking doctors! You didn't do your job, and his cancer came back. You're all assholes. I hate you all! You're all worthless, and your medical degrees are worthless, and everything is worthless."

I screamed on and on across the Bay Bridge and into San Francisco traffic. After parking at my destination, my tears erupted, and I wept and wept. After cathartic screams and tears, I felt calm once again; I put on my game face and dropped off scans that I believed would only bring more grave news.

Three months later, on a sunny fall morning, as I gathered clumps of Rob's hair off the bathroom floor, he called out to me. Rushing into our bedroom, I found him atop our bed, hollow-eyed, his gray skin belying his twenty-six years. His pelvic bones and ribs stretched over his paper-thin skin, and wasted muscles hung on hairless limbs. A spider web of blackened veins ran down his white, stick-like arms where caustic drugs had flowed from IVs. Encased in chemotherapy pain, his 120-pound, skeletal frame barely dented our mattress. He resembled a concentration camp victim; cancer was his concentration camp.

Two-year-old Claire toddled into our bedroom, happy to "see Daddy, see Daddy."

"Get her out of here!" Rob commanded with quickened anger before vomiting into a bowl.

I saw Claire's wide, uncomprehending eyes, and my heart shattered. Weary, Rob lay his balding head back on his pillow as I grabbed the vomit bowl and took Claire's hand.

"Come on, baby," I said, gently leading her out of the bedroom. *Thank God, she'll never remember this. Thank God for small favors.*

When I returned, I found Rob in unbearable pain, bent into a fetal position. "Please take the kids to stay with a grandmother. It's too much for me."

Despite my fatigue from heavy emotions day after day, I left our bedroom to pack their stuff. After buckling our infant and toddler into their car seats, I drove to Mom's house, lost and exhausted. Then, I turned around and drove home to take care of Rob.

Later that night, the worst moment in my marriage happened. Rob called out to me until I woke up.

"Can you go sleep in Hunter's room? I can't stand having anyone next to me."

Feeling broken, I crawled out of our bed and curled into the guest bed. Was this it? The last night I would ever sleep with him? Was he going to die?

After a restless sleep, I awoke to his loud moans. I ran into our bedroom, tripping in the darkness.

"Please, baby, take me to Emergency." Rob despised the hospital.

"Are you sure?"

"Yes, take me."

As I sped down the freeway on the clear night, a luminous full moon rose, carved with a small, dark, reddish sliver. "Oh my God. Look at that, Rob. A total eclipse of the moon is starting soon."

Rob groaned.

Emergency personnel placed Rob on a gurney in a hallway as we waited for a room to open. And we waited some more—more waiting upon more useless waiting.

By two a.m., I lost it. I ran down to the nurses' station and interrupted their conversation, yelling, "Hey! You guys gotta help my husband. He's been waiting in the hallway for a long time. He has cancer!" I paced back and forth as their faces told me they had forgotten about him. "Help him, please!"

After his quick admission, Rob dozed on a white bed in a white gown, connected to a hydrating IV bag, his face at last peaceful.

Squeezing his hand, I watched him breathe until three-thirty a.m., overcome with worry that if I left, I'd never see him again.

At the hospital exit, I stood frozen with fear, unable to enter the shadowy parking garage alone. Italy had followed me, and now it awaited me in the dark, demanding more than ever that I keep constant watch in my unsafe world.

At Security, I asked for an escort to my car.

As I waited, Dr. Antonini, one of Rob's nicer physicians, walked outside and looked at the sky.

I followed him through the door and asked, "Looking at the eclipse?"

"Yeah, it's just ending. See it?" A slice of red shadow nipped into the moon's bright face.

"I saw it rising when we came here and showed it to Rob, but all he could say was 'Uh.'"

After a skinny kid in a uniform walked up, the doctor smiled and said goodnight. I turned to my escort. "Sorry, I don't like dark places."

"Neither do I."

"Especially tonight with a full moon eclipse."

"Really?" he said, aiming his flashlight beam at my car handle as I slipped my key into the lock.

"Yeah, it's an old wives' tale. Intense things happen during eclipses."

Safely in my car, I laid my forehead against the steering wheel. *How did we land here, trapped in an unknown territory, dark and unmapped?* I hated standing by as sinister shadows sliced apart our lives. But there was nothing I could do.

In the morning, Rob's mother came over to join me and visit Rob. As we got into my car to head to the hospital, she said, "Honey, let's stop at church to pray for Rob."

On a weekday our parish church was vacant; we knelt in a pew before the altar. I folded my hands to pray as my head dropped in despair.

I'm losing him. I can't stand this. Why does it have to be Rob? My kids need their dad. Please, God, help him, so his kids will grow up with their dad and remember him.

After praying, we left our pew, and I absentmindedly followed my mother-in-law down the wide church aisle. A strong, clear voice in my head said, "He's going to be okay."

It sounded like the voice of Jesus. But how? How could Jesus be speaking to me like that, with such obvious clarity? The voice felt so true, so real. I shook my head in disbelief, wondering what had just happened. I had never heard anything so true before. This secret knowledge filled me with a sense of peace unlike I'd ever known. And it ensured me that our ordeal would end. I wasn't going to lose Rob. He would survive.

From that moment, convinced of the voice and its truth, after any bad news, a depressing test result, or a new surgery, I tamped down my panic by recalling that voice. Instead of allowing my dread for our future to choke me, I let that voice thrive inside me. When the oncologist offered little hope for Rob's survival, I reminded myself about the voice.

Then, he said that Rob's odds of survival were "Fifty-fifty. Maybe."

And I let that voice respond, "No, I disagree. It's 100 percent."

Tumultuous storms of Rob's chemo and eleven hospitalizations rocked our year. And, as we reached the end of his treatment, money grew tight. One day, I walked out to our mailbox to find that a new storm had blown in, our property tax bill.

With Rob on disability, I didn't have the money to pay it. *Good God, we could lose our home.*

I hated to call Dad, but I had no choice. "Could you lend me the money to pay our property taxes? With Rob not working, we don't have it."

"No problem."

"I'll pay you back, Dad, I promise. When this is all over."

"Nah, Lenore, you keep it."

I croaked a thank you. I would repay him—I owed him so much more.

After eight grueling months since Rob began chemotherapy, the day came when his chemo nurse administered his last dose.

I sat on his bed, saying, "It's finally over!"

Rob only gave me a wan smile, the chemo robbing everything from him, especially joy.

"Now our normal life starts," I said with a hug. When I pulled away, I realized Rob had a very long physical recovery ahead of him, so I added, "I'll get you fattened up."

His oncologist walked in and stood at the head of Rob's bed. "Okay, Rob, you are good to go," he said. "Before you leave, stop at the nurses' station to make an appointment for your final scan."

A final scan? What final scan? I hadn't allowed myself to think Rob might still be in danger—that they might not have gotten all the cancer.

Two weeks later, I found myself on the phone all evening with friends and family as the bearer of bad news; Rob didn't feel like talking and had retreated to our bedroom to watch TV. His latest scan revealed that the chemotherapy hadn't killed the mass behind his heart.

Everyone called, each shell-shocked after hearing our news. I answered their identical questions, twisting the phone cord with my fingers and pacing the kitchen as far as the cord allowed.

"Yes, that mass is there," I answered on autopilot. "Well, it's a serious chest surgery . . . No, they won't know anything until the biopsy's done . . . They'll know the treatment once they know what's going on . . . Yes, we got your card. Very kind . . . Thank you for your prayers; we really appreciate them."

By eight o'clock, feeling bereft, I took the phone off the hook, out of energy. I plopped down on the bed next to Rob.

He had nothing to say. I had nothing to say. We fell asleep early, exhausted.

Two weeks later, on the morning of Rob's chest surgery to remove the mass, I rushed to the hospital in the pre-dawn darkness to hold his hand in the elevator going down to the surgical suite. Due to construction, the hospital lobby also functioned as a surgical waiting room, an apt setting for my chaos and confusion. In a daze, I got lost among construction barriers and detour signs.

But I got to him in time. "I love you," I whispered, but Rob had already faded away. My heart tripped inside my chest as the professionals took over to whisk him through double doors.

Those same goddamn double doors where I met Dr. Abad after Rob's first surgery.

Down the hall, I spotted the little room where this misery began two years earlier. I closed my eyes, trembling at that painful memory.

Standing alone, I drowned in pain as tears dripped off my face. When a passerby noticed them, I held my head high, unashamed. In the waiting room, I found my subdued father; Mom was at my house having spent the night before babysitting our little ones.

Tight with anxiety, I took a seat.

"How's he doing?" Dad asked.

"He's all right. They don't know how long this will take."

Dad circled the room, picked up a newspaper, studied it, and then dropped it on a table.

As a kid, I was fascinated by Dad's pacing ritual; he'd come home, weary from a day in the trenches, and circle the room to unwind himself after work, picking up and then putting down mail until easing into his chair. I imagined him as a jungle cat, circling and flattening the grass before settling down.

His waiting room circles narrowed until he sat beside me, too distraught to make small talk. I understood. Small talk required a Herculean effort.

I squirmed in my rigid plastic chair—nothing but more waiting.

Dad's quiet presence brought me great relief.

When this new cancer recurrence terrified me more than chemo, when I couldn't stand watching Rob suffer a second longer, Dad had believed in me and told me how strong I was. "It's guts," he'd said. "You've always had guts."

But I got my guts from him.

Unafraid of launching into battle with me, Dad sat with me in the waiting room as the hours passed. As I studied worn women's magazines, restlessness overtook me. *Their helpful hints can't help me now. Nope, you can't sugarcoat this reality.*

Incapable of bearing any more bad news, I was happy to take a break from the endless waiting—I left for my therapy appointment, which I'd purposely scheduled during Rob's surgery.

Upstairs in the therapist's office, I ranted and dumped my anguish onto her lap, rocking with the rage I refused to show the world. Daily, I'd buried my fears behind a heavy mask while slowly losing the man I loved. Every night, feeling spent, I'd trembled in bed with nowhere to hide from a world so brutal.

The therapist sat with me, listening and gently guiding, reminding me to breathe and telling me my fear and pain were normal.

As I stood to leave, I lost my balance and forced myself upright. Morose thoughts circled inside my head. *The surgeon will appear in his scrubs to tell us about the mass. His cancer has spread. He needs more chemo. I'm losing him forever.*

Suddenly, my face and hands grew icy. *That voice I'd heard in church wasn't real.*

I plodded downstairs, staring at the ground and bracing myself for the surgeon's news. I searched for Dad's steady presence.

Dad stood up and pulled me into a hug. "Lenore, it's all gone!" he said, his eyes bright.

"What? What do you mean?"

"The surgeon, you just missed him. He said there was nothing there."

Rob's mom Virginia, who had joined Dad, smiled through her tears, saying, "Honey, it's gone!"

She hugged me, and I hugged her back, feeling like a robot going through the motions.

"No tumor, only scar tissue," said Dad. "The scan must've shown a shadow."

I shook my head in disbelief. "A shadow?" I rasped. Unable to breathe, my head got heavy, and I sank into a chair, stupefied.

"Lenore, it was just scar tissue from the chemo. It's gone!" said Dad.

"Honey, Rob's going to be all right," said Rob's mom, glowing with joy.

"He's going to be all right," I intoned. I put my face in my hands, unable to wrap myself around their words. *That voice had been real. It had told me the truth.* A frisson of joy ran up my spine.

Then, Dad said, "We've got to call everyone, Lenore, and let them know."

After the three of us made happy calls to our loved ones, Dad suggested we celebrate.

"I know a place right across the street," I said. "Maybe they're open." The town's fanciest restaurant was a clubby place with red leather booths and tables covered in snowy white tablecloths and adorned with roses in silver vases. We stumbled from the morning sun into a dark, womb-like bar and sat at a low table.

"Champagne!" said Dad to the barman.

At eleven-thirty in the morning.

Virginia and I couldn't stop laughing. Tears ran down our faces, and Dad shook his head. "What's a celebration without champagne!"

"I can't believe it," I said in disbelief, amazed how life could plummet you into the darkest place only to shoot you straight into an open sky.

The clank of an iced champagne bucket broke my thoughts, and the bartender popped our celebratory bottle.

"Neither can I, but thank God!" said Dad. "Here's to Rob and his health."

We clinked our glasses.

"We have to have a Mass said to thank God for this," said my mother-in-law, her eyes shiny with joy.

Sucking down my first glass too fast, I swiveled in my red leather chair, delirious, saying, "Mmm, *effervescent*."

I didn't feel our first bottle of champagne—my emotions burned up the alcohol.

Dad signaled the barman and said, "Another one, please."

After our third bottle, despair released its sharp teeth on my heart.

So, this is how it feels to be free.

We ordered thick steaks and guzzled more champagne. Our raucousness attracted attention as the business lunch crowd filed in and filled the red leather booths.

"Oh, I have to go," I said, trying to stand up. "Rob should be waking up now."

I walked back across the street and slipped into Recovery, where I found Rob sleeping, tubes snaking out from under his blankets. I held his hand, waiting for him to wake and wondering if this new, uncharted territory would be worth its toll. We had learned so much about how illness and trauma can slice you open, exposing raw parts of yourself you didn't know existed.

And yet, looking back at my life, I felt like it had all been worth it: diving headfirst into adulthood, marrying right out of college, having Claire so soon, and embracing those precious three weeks to conceive Hunter.

Rob began to stir, squeezing my hand and opening his eyes.

"There's no tumor, honey," I said, my words slurring. "He didn't find anything. No cancer. You're going to be okay."

"Oh, that's good," he murmured. "Now I'll get to see our kids grow up."

24

BATTLE-HARDENED

Months later, on a chilly winter night, we lay in bed as Rob studied the surgical scars on his twenty-seven-year-old torso. We had steered out of the rutted, gutted side of the road and gotten our lives back on track. After almost two years, victorious after our cancer war, our family of four remained whole.

"Do you still want this broken-down old man?" Rob asked me.

"I do." I leaned in to kiss his cheek. "You're not broken. Look at you. You've gained some weight, and you've got stubble growing on your scalp. And now you're back at work."

"Yeah, work makes me feel normal again." He loved his job engineering the manufacture of cables, overseeing his draftsmen, and working alongside the union guys on the floor.

"We're just battle-hardened, that's all," I said. "We'll get used to normal life again. That takes time."

"And you were strong enough to take charge," Rob added. "You handled the caretaking, childcare, and household, all without a man to help you.

Our young family is now whole and Rob lets me take his picture after his hair grew back.
Image courtesy of the author's collection.

You're strong, capable, and loving. And you had the spirit to move forward like I had never seen before."

I cuddled close to him. "Thanks. I had some growing up to do. I mean, after this nightmare, all those little annoyances, you know, like a check lost in the mail or a broken garage door, they mean nothing to us."

Though crushed by our monumental San Francisco Bay Area mortgage, we earned our peaceful, boring life under the suburban oaks of a leafy town. As a stay-at-home mom with two toddlers sixteen months apart, I savored my busy life.

Yes, we had won our cancer war. But I knew life wouldn't magically snap back to normal. Just like my life didn't snap back to normal when I returned from Italy. Eventually, my life got better after meeting Rob, having our kids, and seeing Rob's clear scans. Yet, depression had its claws in me, and I found myself waiting for more bad news.

That winter, record-setting rainstorms plagued California. On soggy mornings, as I began my day of caring for our young ones, I listened to the news. Houses slid down Sausalito's steep hills, and in Malibu and Santa Cruz, homes collapsed into the sea.

I got tired of waking every morning and falling asleep every night to a rainstorm. Alone all day, I dragged myself around as if plowing through water. Mail stacked up in the mailbox, and phone calls went unreturned. I stayed indoors all day and slept too much, yet I battled exhaustion. Our cupboards grew empty; I couldn't muster the energy to drag my poor toddlers through pouring rain to the grocery store.

Amid my malaise, my pen scratched angrily in my journal to document irritating slights, such as a grocery clerk's impatience with my kids. Any tiny cut swelled into an uncontainable outrage. I needed to meet with my therapist again.

After shedding my raincoat and folding my umbrella, I sat on my therapist's couch, begging her to tell me why I was so depressed. "What's wrong with me? My life is great," I said.

"Sometimes stress keeps our minds and nervous systems hyper-vigilant, which can be draining," she said. "Then we become too angry or exhausted with life."

"But I sleep all the time." I stared at her, uncertain, waiting for more.

"That's because your sleep isn't restorative," she said. "You need time to heal from such a traumatizing time. You probably have PTSD."

The therapist explained that Rob's cancer had torpedoed me and how, after such a traumatizing experience, depression and PTSD can appear. In fact, they can go hand in hand.

I hadn't considered that. I'd been too occupied with taking care of everybody.

She pulled out a pad and pen to write an antidepressant prescription for me. "You should be feeling better within a couple of months."

Driving to the sitter's to pick up my kids, I absorbed her words. I could see how my traumatization had grabbed hold of my heart and mind. Rob was traumatized, too. "*Do you still want this broken-down old man?*"

But mine went deeper—all the way back to when I was nineteen. I never told my therapist about the rape, believing I was over it. I had been lying to myself for years about how it wasn't a big deal. Yet I still carried that burden inside; I'd unconsciously shoved those memories away and given all my attention to my family. Wasn't that the best way to move forward?

After Italy, I had lived underwater, immersed in PTSD. And I wasn't just underwater. Our cancer ordeal over two years hit me harder than I'd realized. I was buried underground with depression, too. It all made sense.

So what do I do? I thought, turning into our driveway after picking up Claire and Hunter. I had no idea. At that moment, I had snacks to make, dinner to cook, diapers to change, and laundry to sort.

On another rainy morning, feeling flat and featureless, I dutifully swallowed the anti-depressant my therapist prescribed, but even after several weeks, the chemicals didn't help.

The winter rains and our darkened house matched my mood. As I stepped into the garage to do laundry, I noticed my white vintage leather suitcase, battered and scarred, stowed high on a shelf. A remnant of Mom's 1953 honeymoon luggage set, and a gift from her, it had been perfect for storing my old journals and letters from college and my Italian year.

I ignored it. But my eyes kept studying it as if the case were beckoning me, daring me to open it and in doing so, open a door to the past I desperately wanted to keep shut. I didn't need to face those old memories. I needed to wash my kids' clothes. I turned back to the laundry.

Vague nausea swelled inside my stomach. Ignoring the case wasn't working.

To hell with the laundry. I can't live like this anymore.

Rain thrummed on the roof as I yanked the suitcase onto the cold floor. Swallowing my ancient shame into a hard place inside, I knelt before it on the hard concrete, and after taking a big breath, I snapped the brass locks open.

Lifting the lid revealed a lavish royal blue lining, unworn and unstained. Inside, nestled with other ephemera, tickets, maps, and brochures, lay my journals, textbooks, notebooks, and letters and postcards sent to and from Italy. I sifted through the materials, testaments to how fast my years of college, marriage, and kids had raced by.

I picked up my Mexico travel journal, written after high school graduation at seventeen after journeying to La Paz, Baja California. I paged through it and read about an isolated, pristine cove, Playa Balandra. Its powdery white sand and watery beauty lay under a blinding desert sun with the Sea of Cortez beyond.

I wearily dropped my body to sit cross-legged, placing my journal back into the suitcase. I had grown up so much since seventeen. At twenty-eight, I was no longer a sheltered, indulged Catholic schoolgirl; the stuff of my adult life included life-threatening cancer and rape.

As rain pounded above me, I stared at the suitcase but did not see it. Instead, a song from Pink Floyd's *The Dark Side of the Moon,* the soundtrack of my Italian year, came to mind. The lyrics of "Uncomfortably Numb" spoke of how the child had grown and the dream was gone.

My dream of becoming a writer was gone.

Reading the American expat writers Hemingway and Fitzgerald had stirred an intense longing to write, travel, and live in foreign places. I'd wanted a creative writer's life. I'd wanted the whole world to open for me.

Yet here I was, sitting on cold concrete in my garage, feeling as sad as the never-ending rainfall thrumming on the roof. *What happened to me?*

Gul happened to me. The hard reality of his sexually violent crime destroyed my adventurousness and ambition as my writing dreams skidded off track. In my vulnerability, I went into flight mode without any wings.

When Rob appeared as my shelter from the storm, I fell hard for him, married him, and had Claire right away. This beautiful path distracted me from dealing with my pain.

After Gul stole my innocence, I allowed him to kill my dream. Why else was I stowing my suitcase out of sight and mind in a dark garage?

My therapist said depression is anger turned inward.

What if I turned that anger back outward and used it for something good? Cancer taught me how short life is. What if I refused to let my dreams die? What if I faced my past instead of running from it?

Imbued with hope, I snapped the locks shut and carried my suitcase into the house but not before I grabbed a notebook from a long-ago journalism class where I met the author Tom Wolfe. I wanted to read about my encounter with this inspiring great American writer, a man I believed was a psychedelic dragon yet turned out to be anything but.

As a seventeen-year-old freshman at the College of Marin, I had excitedly signed up for Journalism 101. The class covered the nascent New Journalism movement currently transcending (and upending) American journalism.

Thrilled to meet my favorite writer, I began searching for him from my classroom window. Where was he? He was late. Where was Tom Wolfe?

My instructor invited the bestselling author and pyrotechnic New

Journalist to speak to us during his book tour swing through San Francisco.

I'd already burned through his pioneering work, *The Electric Kool-Aid Acid Test*, which chronicled the Bay Area's counterculture movement and the LSD-fueled adventures of author Ken Kesey and his Merry Pranksters. And I'd pored over all of Wolfe's *Rolling Stone* pieces in the college library.

From the window, I searched for a wild-eyed, hirsute, tie-dyed hippie, but my first sight of Wolfe exploded all my expectations in a nanosecond.

Walking toward me was—a dandy.

On a winter morning, Wolfe strolled through the campus in an impeccable, tailored white suit. Cut in the Savile Row manner, the suit had a single coat button that nipped in his waist; his shirt had a crisp, high collar; and his silk tie and pocket handkerchief matched, both ice cream yellow and peony pink. Cufflinks adorned his stiff white shirt cuffs, and in one hand, he held a gold-tipped cane.

Students swirled by, ignoring the man dressed in a three-piece suit like their uncool fathers, ignoring the writer who had coined the seventies as "The Me Decade."

When this vanilla apparition entered our classroom, I felt confused and leaned forward in my seat.

Kind, courtly, and humble, Wolfe listened to our instructor's introduction. He spoke about his manifesto, *The New Journalism*, an anthology of his cohorts Joan Didion, Hunter S. Thompson, and Truman Capote, among others.

After questions from my class, it was photo time; Wolfe posed like an expert, sitting on the edge of a desk and crooking an ankle over a knee to reveal bright-colored socks and gleaming leather shoes.

He knew the right pose, this man in full, and once the shutter snapped, he dematerialized from my classroom. In his charged wake, he left a new, insecure writer spellbound, stunned, and speechless.

A famous writer whom I worshipped had spoken to me.

I hadn't heard a single word.

Luckily, I had recorded his clever, surprising writing advice in my class notes. He'd given us anarchic advice, such as inserting myself, the reporter, into my articles, which is a cardinal sin in journalism. He advised repeating the same words over and over: "And allow your prose to sing and bathe the reader in Technicolor explosions and staccato glory."

After meeting that renegade, something physically moved inside my gut; my life broke open, exploding from black and white into the riotous colors of my creativity.

Stuffing my notebook into my backpack, I raced outside to lift my head to the azure sky above as clarity opened my mind.

I was going to be a writer. Right now.

After twelve years of Catholic education encased in a uniform, I freed myself to express my creativity and adventurousness. From that moment, I found myself dancing at a club in Sausalito's Gate Five among the pirates squatting in decrepit houseboats and unseaworthy crafts. Or I collected native plant samples on Mount Tamalpais with Jackson and pressed them into my journal. I learned the messy art of ceramics and took a field trip to Arizona's Navajo and Hopi reservations with my anthropology class.

And I wrote down every detail.

25

TRAVEL WRITER

After all these years, could I return to myself and develop my writing craft, as Wolfe advised?

If I was going to become a writer, I had to start writing. After corralling my two little ones I went to an art store for pens and notebooks.

I wanted to start journaling again, writing down what we'd been through, writing away my demons, and maybe lifting my depression.

I bought a large black artist's sketchbook and two fancy ink pens before heading home.

On our back patio, my pen poised above a blank page as I listened to Claire and Hunter playing, shaded by tall redwoods and laurel trees, I wished to capture moments of our children's joy. Words poured onto the page. I wrote about three-year-old Claire as she danced around her baby brother and me:

> She is a sprite, an elf, a fairy maiden with jewel-like green eyes, ivory skin, and hair gilded by the sun. In her lilting voice, she asks for Mommy and then dances away to change her clothes again. My Claire.

I hooked my arm over the back of my patio chair, feeling more optimistic after renewing my old writing habit. Our little family had moved forward fortuitously because Rob had survived, and we appreciated the simple joys of our life.

Tomorrow, I decided, we would go to story time at the library so I could check out more books by great travel writers, such as Paul Theroux, to read during naptimes.

That evening, with Rob recovered and our lives now peaceful, we put our kids to bed and retired to our bedroom to watch our favorite travelogue, *Great Railway Journeys of the World*, hosted by erudite British travel journalists.

Inspired by the show, I had a sudden realization. I said to Rob, "I'm never going to let my life spin away from me again. I want to be a travel writer. But I don't know where to start."

Rob pointed to my stack of travel books on my nightstand and said, "Look at all those books. You're obsessed with travel writing. And life's short, Lenore. So focus. Just move forward and make it happen."

"Yeah, the time to do it is now. But with two toddlers, how? How do I find the time and money to travel and write?"

He leaned close to me, saying, "Trust yourself. You'll figure it out."

"You're right. After thinking about doctors and tests and surgeries for so long, thinking about this goal feels very luxurious."

I picked up Robyn Davidson's inspiring book, *Tracks: A Woman's Solo Trek Across 1700 Miles of Australian Outback*, off my nightstand and read about this courageous Aussie's improbable journey across Australia with her camels. Her story planted a profound belief inside that I could achieve impossible goals too.

The next day, I scratched a plan out in my notebook as pasta boiled on the stove.

Rob can watch the kids on Sundays, enabling me to nurture my travel writing ambitions by studying a copy of Writer's Market *and the* San Francisco Examiner *Sunday travel section. Once a week, I'll pack the kids into the car for library story time. As they listen to, say,* Madeline, *I'll study glossy travel magazines and research the craft of travel writing or how to market my work.*

I set my pen down. Yes, that could work. It's enough for now.

Rob arrived home from work, saying, "I got that desk from the plant for you. It's oak from the forties. And a chair, too."

I thanked him as he hauled an old wooden desk inside and pushed it into a corner of our family room.

The next morning, my kids lay on the floor around my feet, drawing, coloring, cutting, and taping their creations onto the sides of my desk as I churned out story pitches to editors.

After the mail arrived, we all went outside to the mailbox where I found a note from the features editor of our local newspaper, *Contra Costa Times*. She liked my pitch on a day trip to Filoli, a 125-acre European-style manor house and gardens built by the Empire Mine's owner. After she published a two-page color spread, she'd need more pitches from me.

I tapped the smooth top of my oaken desk, saying, "You've brought me good luck."

I worked long hours, researching unusual local adventures. I sent pitches to travel editors about horseback rides to Muir Beach's Pelican Inn pub for cold pints of ale or exploring the Victorian splendor of San Francisco's Conservatory of Flowers. Plenty of rejections crossed my desk, but then, editors started sending assignments along with their deadlines.

I rocked at my desk anxiously. How was I going to meet all these deadlines? *I guess I won't be sleeping much.*

Yet I wanted to push myself. I needed one audacious idea. And that idea appeared while I pushed Hunter's stroller past a travel agency displaying a large poster of Australia. Since reading *Tracks*, I'd been fascinated with that antipodean country, and now that poster seeded my plan.

Back at home, I dove into *Writer's Market*, my mind swimming with possibilities. I created a plan, and my excitement instilled me with inner energy. I read every book on Australia in the library, researching destinations and story angles. Soon, I'd collected several story assignments.

One day, as Rob came home from work and threw a pile of mail on the counter, I said, "Guess what? Remember how I contacted the Australian Tourist Commission after getting all those assignments?"

"Yeah," he said, looking up as he sorted mail.

"Well, they offered me a free business-class ticket to a new airport in Cairns, Queensland. They also threw in a train ride through the Kuranda rainforest and stays at an outback station and a luxury island resort on the Great Barrier Reef."

"Oh my God, that's great," said Rob. "I want to go with you!"

"I want you to go with me, too. But how? We don't have the money."

"Or maybe we do," he said, after pulling something from an envelope. He waved an unexpected tax refund check in the air, asking, "Sure you don't want to replace that old living room couch instead?"

I laughed out loud. "You know my answer."

Two months later, as I relaxed in bed, sipping my morning coffee, Rob tossed the Sunday newspaper on our bed.

"It's here!" he said in a singsong. "I found it. Look, Lenore." He held up my cover story gracing the front page of the *San Francisco Examiner*'s Sunday travel section. I grabbed it and searched for my byline above an article on California's Gold Country. I leaned back on my pillows, speechless.

"Wow, you did it," said Rob.

"Oh my God, Rob, do you know that today, one million readers will read this?"

And it was worth all the effort—the long hours, little sleep, and messy house.

26

IMPOSSIBLE DOORS
AND FALSE MASKS

After I visited and wrote about Australia, I grew as a travel writer, and my byline appeared in newspapers, airline in-flights, guidebooks, travel magazines, and blogs. I had taken the steps to follow my dream of travel writing, and it got me outside of myself and into the world.

As the years flew by, I grew a bit closer to the woman I had wished to become when I first took off for Italy. Though I had grown stronger, I sometimes struggled with my old compulsion to escape when life got tough.

But one day, I found myself wrestling with returning to Italy with Rob. I wavered as I considered sabotaging the trip with a conveniently ill-timed work assignment even if it disappointed Rob. The pull to escape was strong but so was my guilt.

The whole idea began one afternoon as I put away groceries in the kitchen. Rob called me from Bologna during a business trip. Now a consulting engineer, he had traveled to Italy with clients to study soap-making machinery for a project. Apparently, the Italians excelled at designing soap machinery as much as they did Ferraris and couture fashion.

"Their machines are as elegant as they are functional," he told me over the phone. "But the Italians weren't ready for us, of course, so we took a day off and decided to visit Venice."

In awe, he described discovering the city's watery beauty for the first time.

"I'm jealous; I've never been there," I said, stowing packages in the freezer. I also felt relief that I hadn't jumped at the chance to join him but stayed safe at home instead.

"But Venice wasn't so fun with a bunch of guys. We'll go back together. It's so romantic, Lenore, and I want to take you there."

Maybe it was time to stop allowing fear to control me. Maybe it was time to go back to Italy. But not alone.

"I'd love going with you. Let's go."

Over the next few months, I made travel plans, poring over maps and guidebooks. But ancient shadows stalked me, so I eliminated Perugia from our itinerary. I booked flights to Milan and train tickets to Venice; that way, I wouldn't disturb the muddy bottom underneath the still waters within me.

Was I still the girl who'd been shattered by sexual violation? Was visiting Italy a good idea? After all, I'd still never confronted my past in therapy. It was too scary.

Nervous about facing my demons yet excited for our adventure, I felt a hint of fear about how this trip could affect me. I told myself I had healed so much since Perugia, building a happy life with Rob. And I loved watching our kids, now teenagers, grow up near the beach in a place as gorgeous as Mill Valley.

During the months leading up to our trip, anticipation and anxiety intertwined in my mind. As a married woman of a certain age, I wondered if Italian men would treat me differently than they had when I was younger. Would I feel less like a target? I hoped traveling with my husband would banish my sense of vulnerability. If I were with Rob, certainly no one would ever yell at me, "Come on, baby, you sleep with me?"

As we strolled alongside the Grand Canal in Venice, La Serenìssima, a once prosperous sovereign republic, I savored my cinnamon gelato cone. Amid buzzing motorboats, splashing waves, and stinking marine fuel, reflections of canal waters danced lithely across the façades of ornate palaces. Venice's serenity soaked into me. Exploring this sumptuous sculpture of an aquatic city with Rob, I discovered the Italy I had imagined at nineteen, a grand Italy, sunlit and astounding in beauty.

I knew we only explored a curated "tourist Italy," far from the raw, unfiltered Italy I had crashed into as a student. The residue of that experience lingered in Venice, surfacing in unexpected ways. Sometimes, I'd pause instinctively before walking into a dark passage, my fear rising, before I'd rationalize it away. The sudden clatter of footsteps on cobblestones made me tense. The smell of damp stone sometimes triggered a pang of dread. I caught myself scanning crowds, unconsciously bracing for something unknown. These strange moments came and went like ghostly echoes, reminders that, though the scenery had changed, parts of me were still entwined in shadows.

As we approached a lineup of gondolas, Rob said, "We've got to take a romantic gondola ride even if it's a touristy thing to do. You negotiate the price."

After I untangled the gondolier's incomprehensible dialect, I got his price. As we floated gracefully through canals past decaying buildings, I grew fascinated with the heavy, ornate waterfront doors, some half-submerged, some forever bricked up, and some splintered and corroded by saltwater. Interestingly, some drowning doors had tall mooring posts nearby as if boarding were possible.

I took too many photos of them. These impossible doors of Venice beguiled me and then opened to a revelation. Weren't they just like the obstacles I faced in Perugia? Those confounding doors and locks? My struggles when the new Italian life I loved fell apart?

Those Venetian doors revealed I had more healing to do. And that made me sad. *How long will it take?*

Bouncing on waves as our gondola glided across the Grand Canal, I smiled at Rob, disguising my thoughts. I couldn't tell him how I found myself pulled between two journeys: one in my enchanting Venetian present with Rob and another deep within my painful Italian past. The inner journey was mine alone; I still honored Rob's request that I not speak to him about that night. When I pushed, needing to connect with him and to release my pain, Rob's sadness and anger, and even a kind of vicarious pain, mirrored my own. So I protected him from the weight I carried, staying silent but churning in resentment beneath the surface.

From a canal, I spied Ca' Macana, a mask-making workshop displaying handmade Venetian masks. As soon as we disembarked our gondola, I pulled Rob's hand to make a beeline to the tiny atelier, walking fast and saying, "We've got to see Ca' Macana."

Beginning in the thirteenth century, masks played starring roles during the Venetian Carnevale party season before Lent. Behind elaborate, gilded, or veiled face masks, Venetians disguised their true identities; a poor man could masquerade as a nobleman or a high-born woman as a libertine. Deeply rooted in the culture, masks erased the constraints of class and public morals while safeguarding reputations.

We dipped inside Ca' Macana to confront a riotous display of masks lining the walls and spilling from tables.

"Oh, they're so beautiful, Rob," I said.

Created from embellished papier-mâché, the masks were painted in rich colors—gold, scarlet, midnight blue, or glossy ebony. Embellished with swooping black feathers, crystals, gold leaf, sequins, and brocade, many masks bore names, such as Bauta, a full-face mask, and Colombina, a woman's half mask. They also portrayed characters, such as Arlecchino, best known as Harlequin, or Larva, "ghost" in Latin. I was attracted to one Larva mask, ghost-white with red lips formed into a Mona Lisa smile and wearing a tricorn hat dripping with iridescent beads.

Wandering around the atelier, my fondness for the Venetians' artful tools of deceit was born. In medieval and Renaissance Venice, laws restricted women's movements, rights, and freedoms. Once Carnevale arrived, a woman could hide her secrets behind her mask and leave her neighborhood during the festivities.

Isn't that what a woman must do in Italy? Hide behind a mask to free herself and enjoy her life? Hadn't I done the same thing to survive in Perugia?

Back then, I wore my mask of confidence to distract myself from my pain, fear, and vulnerability. Now in Venice, I masked my emotions when I caught the sight of a lone man standing in an archway, which transported me back to my anguished past twisting around me like a rope.

I bore burdens Rob never wanted to talk or hear about. But what about me? Why did I protect him? Why couldn't I share all of this with him—he was my husband! The greatest irony was that I was ready to talk. But he wouldn't.

Wishing to feel safe, strong, and healed, I wanted to remove my mask in Venice, and I hoped we'd find time to talk. On this trip, it was just the two of us without the teenage clamor and activity in the house. Maybe we'd find a moment. Maybe I could convince him to hear me.

We left the shop and walked, hand in hand, to a nearby canal. Watching the gray-green water running below us, I ached to tell Rob how, in Venice, I danced between light and dark and beauty and pain. But I fell too easily into my old habit of escaping my feelings and went silent.

I pondered the impossible-to-open doors shutting in my suppressed pain. If I plunged through a half-submerged door inside my soul, I'd get snagged by my trauma because parts of that vulnerable girl still lived inside me.

As visceral memories cropped up, I felt forced to confront, for the first time in years, how deeply the rape had devastated me at nineteen. Feeling profound compassion for that young woman, I believed the only thing that would've been worse for her was murder.

Yet, returning to Italy taught me how healing resembles the peeling of layers from an onion. Once you remove one layer, you find a deeper layer to heal. Over the years, I had transformed, bit by bit, and then, upon peeling a new layer, I'd regress a bit. Like the canals of Venice, over the years, my journey of healing from sexual violence had meandered, snaked, and curved around me. Maybe my journey would never end.

27

HARD CHOICES IN ORVIETO

My Venetian trip with Rob allowed me to enjoy both the sweetness and bitterness of Italy. When I accepted that truth, I felt less dogged by distress. I became more willing to see recovery as a journey, not a straight path.

So, a year later, when my brother Angelo decided to get married in Orvieto, off to Italy I flew, feeling confident about my trip since I'd be with my loved ones and Dad. But not with Rob, who chose to stay home with our teenagers, saying, "Great, your brother won't get married in San Francisco, so *I* have to go to Italy." I had to wonder if this was his attempt to keep me from bringing up my past again.

On an Umbrian spring morning, I joined a mob of family, friends, and Italian relatives converging on the hill town of Orvieto. Every day, we gathered in a café for our morning coffee. I sat, smiling, surrounded by people who made Italy feel bright and shiny, like a happy Italy, not like the country where gloom had stalked me.

I felt as though I was visiting Italy like a normal person.

All together for the first time in our sunny home country, we engaged in a beautiful reunion.

I bantered with them and laughed at jokes over my cappuccino and croissant. As more relatives and friends arrived, Italians and Americans, I smiled and asked questions with genuine curiosity and interest: "Who's arriving today? What's going on with the wedding? What are you wearing?"

Then, everyone began tossing out ideas for day trips to take after the wedding.

"Let's go to Assisi . . . Okay, we'll share a car with you . . . We're going shopping in Deruta for ceramics . . . Oh, we want to go to Perugia."

I stared into my cup, and Mom noticed. "Well, Lenore?" she asked, wiping cappuccino foam from her lips. "Aren't you visiting Perugia?"

My head jerked up. *Oh, God, no.* I bashed the idea of returning to Perugia. "No, Assisi," I answered.

"But don't you want to see Perugia again? I thought you'd like to go back."

My happiness faded as I stiffened in my small café chair. *Poor Mom. She had no idea.* Why return to my former haunt? I feared my traumatic memories might reawaken the ghost of the girl within me.

"Nope," I said. "I already lived there for a year, but I'd love to see Assisi again. It's such a peaceful place." I finished my breakfast in stony silence.

I was excited to visit the serene hometown of my favorite saint, the peaceful Saint Francis. I had learned his history during my trips to Assisi with my Italian girlfriends. The nuns had never taught me that, as a teenaged soldier fighting in Assisi's war with Perugia, the saint had been captured, held hostage, and imprisoned in a dank dungeon for a year. Since then, Saint Francis's legacy of peace had resonated within me. I tossed down the last of my coffee and smiled at Mom, my mask firmly attached to my face.

"I think Assisi would be really cool to visit, Mom."

"Great. And don't forget," she said, "we are all eating together this afternoon."

Later that day, Mom and Dad hosted a grand pranzo, or midday meal, with my brothers, my sister, her husband, the bridal couple, relatives, and friends. As we passed platters of roast rabbit and handmade gnocchi, I glanced down the long, bustling table feeling a real joy. I loved sitting next to Dad on a wooden chair, listening to him joking in rudimentary Italian and making the Italians roar with laughter.

Experiencing Italy with Dad again for the first time since my student days brought a deep meaning to my journey. Being with him evoked happy memories of when my exciting new Italian life first began—a moment filled with boundless possibilities and the warmth of his pride and love.

In the late afternoon, everyone miraculously ended up at the same gelateria, tucked away off the central Piazza del Duomo in the historical center. Sitting at outside tables with my parents, the about-to-be-married couple, and other relatives and friends, I translated the names of the gelato flavors inside: "blackberry and chestnut," "Grandmother's Cream," and "Bewitched Ricotta."

Grace and I went inside to search the long glass case holding psychedelically colorful tubs of handcrafted gelato. Grace chose the poetically named "Flower of Almond Milk" mixed with sour cherries.

Then I spied the sign for Bacio, a gelato laced with Perugia's famous hazelnut and chocolate kisses. My face tightened. I hated seeing reminders of that town.

Jesus, why did Angelo have to get married so close to Perugia? And why am I so angry about it? I'm not in danger anymore.

I let my sadness and anger go, distracted by my cinnamon gelato's heavenly deliciousness. It was never available in US gelato places, so I ordered a double cone to indulge in one of the pleasures dating from my year abroad. Some things are worth remembering.

The morning after the wedding, we took off on our day trips. I joined the group that included Grace and Mom heading to beautiful Assisi. They were hell-bent on shopping for local ceramics and crafts. A bit more touristy since I'd last been there, Assisi looked the same, nestled under Monte Subiaso, which I remembered as snow-capped during a cold winter long ago.

I excused myself from the shoppers, saying, "I'll meet you guys up top at the basilica."

I started uphill on Assisi's narrow streets toward the Basilica of Saint Francis, passing shops displaying rosaries, crucifixes, and tourist knick-knacks. Then I stopped, realizing I was lost in the hill town's convoluted streets.

Oh no, I have to backtrack. I can't follow any roads leading to Perugia.

I turned around, finally found Via San Francesco, and continued walking toward warm memories of my happy times there laughing with Chiara, Lina, and Stefania, lounging on the basilica's wide front lawn and smiling for snapshots.

And nearby Perugia? There lived cold memories of imprisonment and my inability to escape. What kept me from leaving all those years ago was a mind so muddled it wouldn't allow me to choose whether to hang on or to bail. If I had bailed, how would Mom and Dad have reacted? Would they have supported me with love? Or gotten angry and accused me of promiscuity? Already so wounded, I knew I couldn't have borne any more wounds.

Now, as I passed the familiar architecture, the rough brick buildings and stone-paved streets snaking through town, I knew any sense memory, a sight, sound, smell, taste, or touch, could shoot me back into my painful past. But I kept climbing.

As I huffed and puffed, in my mind, I tried reconciling two opposing ideas and two places simultaneously.

Assisi and Perugia.

Peace and prison.

Why hold onto both at the same time? It's crazy making. Hopeless. Like Assisi's steep, stony streets, healing can be complicated and nonlinear, rife with setbacks. Frustrated with my futile struggles, I decided to end this cycle.

I decided to simply enjoy my journey.

I climbed Via San Francesco until the Basilica of Saint Francis appeared with its Gothic ivory-colored stone face standing against a clear sky. *There it is! Ah, it's still so beautiful.*

I sat on the grass to take it all in while catching my breath, happy to be back in Assisi amid pleasant memories. The spring sun warmed my face, and my body felt solid and supported on the earth. In peaceful Assisi, too much beauty surrounded me to waste a moment thinking about my sad history.

And, at the end of my journey that day, I accepted this small victory.

28

THE WARRIOR
WAS RESTING

Another blow rocked my world just as life moved along with my family
and my writing. This time, it wasn't Rob's health. Our kids were fine. I was
feeling better—finally.

One day, Rob answered his phone, listened silently, and immediately
handed it to me, his brown eyes soft with grief.

"It's your dad. It doesn't sound good."

Shaking, I listened to my sibling relate how a simple cardiac procedure
went scarily sideways and Dad's heart began to dance erratically. The clinic
checked him into the hospital for observation and to figure out what was
going on.

Devastated, I rushed to the hospital.

When he was well enough to be discharged, he began his recovery in
my childhood home. I walked into his bedroom and slumped into a chair
next to his bed. He looked terrible, his face gray and drawn, and my heart

ached. Watching my father wither like a leaf about to fall to earth, I couldn't help acknowledging that death drew near.

He didn't talk much, but I overflowed with happiness to be near him. To pass the time, I went through family photo albums, paging through years of Dad's photos of family parties, weddings, Holy Communions, and holidays. For over fifty years, he documented his family life and our childhoods in organized and labeled photo albums.

"Look, Dad, here's a beach party at Tahoe with everyone," I said.

"Those were fun," he rasped. He studied it for a moment and lay back on his pillow, silent.

"Ah, look at me." I pointed to a snapshot he had taken of me at sixteen with the blue of Lake Tahoe beyond. In nature, near the water, I sat at a picnic table during a barbecue with other families, smiling at Dad. "Look how the barbecue smoke split the rays of the sun. It created a halo around my wet hair."

"Yeah," he said too softly.

I searched for a flash of Dad's usual joie de vivre. The warrior was resting, preparing to lay down his weapons and slip away from me forever.

Grief-stricken, I put the album down. Could I handle it? Perhaps. I'd been through so much. But having been raised by an always-present and supportive father, I felt losing Dad would send me sliding out of control down a steep gravel road. How could I live without his sense of humor, wisdom, and groundedness? How could I live without him in my life?

He had always been there for me. I was the one who always left. My guilt pierced me—I left him for Italy, then for college at Davis, and later when I married. But Dad never left me. But now, Dad would be leaving me forever. And soon.

I felt bereft about staying only a week, but a deadline loomed for a Las

Vegas guidebook I had contracted to write. As I packed, Mom reassured me, saying, "Don't worry, Lenore, he'll be okay."

No one else seemed to know he'd be gone soon. Everyone acted as if he were just getting over a bad flu. *I* knew. On his nightstand lay *Confessions*, Saint Augustine's spiritual biography about his sinful youth and getting right with God. I shut my eyes against the wave of overwhelming sadness crashing inside my heart.

When I kissed him goodbye, we exchanged knowing looks; *this goodbye could be our last.*

I knew.

He knew, too.

I saw it in his eyes.

29

A DIFFERENT KIND OF INVISIBLE

After my troubled week with Dad, I immediately re-entered my distracting travel-writing life. To research my Las Vegas guidebook, I drove across the Mojave Desert but fretted about Dad's frailty during my long drive.

Thankfully, Vegas intervened, especially when I found myself speeding a Ferrari F430 GT around a racetrack with an Italian instructor in my passenger seat. Electric thrills vibrated up and down my spine as I gunned that perfect machine.

After I turned in my guidebook, an adventure travel magazine assigned me to write about Belize. Rob decided to join me on this trip as I researched the Central American country.

When a girlfriend learned that I'd be visiting the jungle town of San Ignacio, she said excitedly, "Oh, Lenore, I met this woman there. I read her book, and Dr. Ariana's just amazing. You've got to read it before you go."

I bought Dr. Ariana's book and found myself tearing through her memoir about her rigorous apprenticeship with the Maya curandero, or

After fording the Macal River on a hand-cranked ferry, Rob grins for my camera.
© Lenore Greiner 2012.

healer, Don Elijio Panti, one of the last living links to ancient Maya healing. For thirteen years, Dr. Ariana had endured an astounding apprenticeship, bushwalking daily for miles, caked in mud, infested with chiggers, and trying to keep up with the small, sturdy Maya as he gathered his plant medicines. While teaching her about the mystical world of healing spirits living within plants and trees, Panti treated alcoholism, diabetes, and post-partum depression. And he stopped dental pain with sap from a tree with ethnobotany's most spectacular name: the Grandfather's Balls Tree.

Dr. Ariana, an American ethnobotanist and doctor of naturopathic medicine, then exported Panti's jungle medicines to US scientists for testing on cancer and the AIDS virus.

I had to meet this spiritual badass. I was eager to learn more about how she pursued her passion and immersed herself in Maya medicine's spiritual realms. Her profound knowledge would bring invaluable depth to my article.

I considered Dr. Ariana a rare bird, the kind of adventurous woman I seldom encountered, and I was excited about meeting her. I scheduled an interview with her, which happened to fall on Halloween.

Lately, I had found myself contemplating the supernatural, consumed with my father's descent toward death. In Catholic school, I'd learned about spirits and guardian angels—even fallen angels called demons. I wondered if other realms existed as well, such as a Maya otherworld?

Once we arrived in San Ygnacio, Belize, I heard Mayan spoken on the street corners. We embarked on local jaunts for my adventure travel assignment. We rode horseback to the ruins of a Maya city, Xunantunich, and climbed a pyramid.

Early the next morning, we embarked on a canoeing trek into Barton Creek Cave, an ancient ceremonial site for Maya gods of the underworld. The supernatural aspect of this trek appealed to me. The cave-obsessed Maya believed all caves were entries to hell where they sacrificed humans and animals and buried high-ranking dead. During sacred rites, while under the influence of hallucinogenic mushrooms, they mutilated their tongues and penises with long obsidian needles.

I assured Rob that our excursion wouldn't include those activities.

Outside the cave, we met our guide, a Belizean of Maya and African descent with the Anglicized name of John Hammond. He stood on a small stone dock alongside canoes floating on a placid spring-fed pond.

"Are we waiting for others?" I asked.

"Only you two. Very few tourists venture inside," he said.

"Really?"

"Yes, the cave's intensity can be so overwhelming that many can't paddle in very far. Sometimes they even jump out of my canoe to swim out of the cave."

I laughed as I boarded his aluminum canoe and waded through a water puddle before taking a seat near the bow. I noticed a car battery atop the bow. *That's strange.*

As Rob boarded the canoe, I noticed wires running from the car battery to a spotlight on the back of the canoe. *Oh my God, the battery is powering the spotlight.*

I jerked my feet out of the puddle and moved away from that fatal arrangement. "What's wrong?" asked Rob.

"I just evaded electrocution," I whispered.

With my death averted, we paddled through a tall slash in a limestone wall draped with curtains of jungle vines and floated upon a slow, tranquil underground river. Soon a wide, two-story-high cavern opened, and I dipped my fingers into icy water. "How far does this river go into the cave?" I asked.

"No one knows," John said. "But a recent mapping expedition went in as far as five miles."

A profound silence engulfed us, more resounding than I'd ever heard. Only the sound of water seeping from the ceiling punctuated the stillness.

We glided underneath limestone bridges and entered cathedral-like caverns through narrow passages and tall tunnels. Bats whooshed above us, and water droplets tinkled and plinked off stalactites. I couldn't shake the feeling that we were intruders in a sacred, otherworldly place.

"The Maya believed their gods and ancestral spirits resided inside Barton Creek Cave," said our guide. Trained and licensed by the tourism board, John knew what he was talking about. I shivered, imagining Maya ancestral spirits watching us in the darkness, their eyes following us as we paddled deeper into the cave.

John swept his powerful spotlight beam over cave walls to the footholds carved by the Maya for climbing high ledges on the cave wall. These held broken pottery smashed by looters over the last thousand years. Then, his spotlight fell upon a human skull and a decapitated skeleton, remnants of a long-ago sacrificial ceremony and signs of past violence.

He illuminated a perfect pot crystallized to a ledge. "This tiny vessel has survived looters for a thousand years."

He told us how it had once overflowed with offerings and stood on a bed of palm leaves and flowers during sacrificial rituals.

When he swung the canoe's bow to face the opposite wall, I sucked in my breath; John's wide beam lit another relic of this surreal and bloody history, a high shelf where a skeleton reposed.

A child-sized skeleton.

They sacrificed a child? Shutting my eyes, I couldn't bear thinking about ripping a child so violently from the world.

We continued through the intense blackness. The air was cool, yet I broke into a sweat.

"A thousand years ago," said our guide, "only royalty, priests, and sacrificial virgins entered this sacred space. After the human sacrifices, the priests left relics behind on altars."

Along with decapitated bodies and severed heads. And blood, lots of blood.

My head spun. I asked John, "Why did they do this?"

"To control the commoners," said John. "As great astronomers, Maya priests predicted eclipses. The king used that secret knowledge to his advantage, saying the gods were angry and the world was ending. Human sacrifices would appease the gods."

He waved his hand in the darkness, saying, "All volunteers and all virgins. Men, women, and children."

Children? I felt sick.

A cloying suffocation grabbed hold of my lungs. To calm myself, I gulped long breaths. I'd been in caves before. What was going on with me? It felt wrong to be in this cave. We didn't belong here.

Yet we kept paddling.

Surrounded by death, I couldn't help thinking about Dad. As my ragged breathing echoed in the cave, I feared the grief awaiting me.

I have to get out of here.

"How far into the cave are we now?" I asked, wearing my mask of confidence.

"Almost a mile," answered John.

We paddled on. In a nonsensical way, the all-encompassing black felt as solid as the rock walls and poised to bury me alive in an underworld. My head spun as if out of control in outer space. Stifling a scream in my throat, I bucked up and kept silent. The only thing to do was wait out this canoe-trip through hell.

On this melancholy river, lost in an underworld, I thought about Dad; I could never escape the pain of losing him. Would it feel just like paddling through a black cave?

I jumped when ice-cold droplets suddenly landed on my skin, droplets the Maya collected as holy water. *Calm down. Calm down. No worries. We're on a cool trip in Central America. Just take it easy and enjoy it.*

But an inner voice disliked those thoughts and shouted, "Get out!" A cold fear bloomed inside me. I shook my head to ignore it and stifle a sense of unwelcome dread. I mustered the courage to ask if we could turn around, head back to the sun. But I didn't want to be a big chicken. I was the one who had landed the assignment for this trip. It had been *my* idea to explore this cave adventure touted by the tourist bureau.

On we paddled.

More skulls. More skeletons.

Anxiety overpowered me, and I wanted out of this cave. We were gliding through a cemetery, and I despised the cruel hush surrounding me. Holding my paddle in a death grip, I struggled with the urge to jump into the cold water and swim a good mile to the cave's mouth. Hell, if physics allowed, I would've dashed across the water's surface like a cartoon character to race outside.

Didn't John say earlier that people had jumped out of his canoe to swim back? Had they heard something, someone yelling, "Get out!" inside their heads, too?

I had never been squeamish. As a kid, I picked up a dead snake and paraded it around the neighborhood kids. But this felt altogether scarier than a dead snake.

Again, I heard a voice inside my head. "Get out! Get out! Get out!"

I've got to get out of here. That voice came from another reality. John talked about how the Maya believed their gods and ancestral spirits lived inside caves, believing they were gates to hell and perfect for sacred rites and human sacrifices.

But then they had left behind skulls, skeletons, blood, smashed pottery, murdered children, death . . .

We paddled on.

The beam briefly fell upon Rob's face, lifted in amazement as we glided past another brutal tableau. I gripped the canoe's gunwales. John's single shaft of light could never overcome the cave's immense blackness or its silent violence.

In the pitch black, I lost control and croaked, "I hate to break it to you, guys, but I can't go any farther. Do you mind if we turn around? Now?"

John accommodated me; he knew I was another casualty of the cave's extreme energy. He said, "You've made it farther than most."

Rob looked at me, puzzled.

"Don't you feel it, too?" I asked.

"Feel what?"

After John turned the bow toward the cave entrance, I couldn't paddle fast enough, driven to tear away from bones and skulls and relics of death rites.

My fright lifted when a pinpoint of daylight appeared ahead and slowly widened. I breathed more freely as I returned to the light and felt as if I had crawled from the seventh violent ring of hell into a sunlit, terrestrial paradise.

Near the cave's mouth, birdsong warbled, and I felt calmer. We floated outside as howler monkeys barked from the treetops. We landed back at the stone dock, where John tied up our canoe and I climbed out and stood up to soak in the sunshine.

"Thanks, John," I said, running my fingers through my hair. "Wow, that cave did me in. I don't know what's going on in there."

"You just witnessed the power of the cave," said John matter-of-factly. He didn't seem shocked, as if everyone had a cave freak-out during their paddle.

In that realm of stone, skulls, and inky, cold water, something invisible made itself known to me. But what? A presence from the Maya underworld? The ghost of someone sacrificed inside the cave?

While caught in my profound sadness about Dad, perhaps surrounding myself with skulls and bones hadn't been such a great idea.

✸

On our ride back to San Ignacio, I had more questions than answers and hoped Dr. Ariana could shed light on Maya spirits and their mystical world.

The next morning, we sped down the Western Highway in a taxi, passing placid cattle in emerald pastures before turning onto a dirt track. We drove into the Maya Mountains and entered a lush landscape, passing a medicine plant trail preserving traditional Maya healing herbs and plants. Then we entered the gate of Dr. Ariana's Ix Chel Research Station, named after the Maya goddess of medicine whom Panti called Lady Rainbow.

As birds trilled, we climbed uphill to a solid Belizean house overlooking the Macal River, once an essential Maya trade route.

An Italian-Assyrian woman originally from Chicago, Dr. Ariana walked out of her home and warmly greeted us. Smiling and serene, she wore slacks, a floral top, and gold hoop earrings. Now in her sixties, this peaceful jungle warrior would've looked perfectly natural pushing a cart in a US grocery store.

She led us around her yellow two-story home to an expansive deck overlooking a grassy slope falling toward the jungle. The faint chatter of chachalaca birds in the river valley beyond broke the morning peace.

Sipping our tea, I asked, "Where did this Maya healing knowledge come from?"

"For any condition Panti treated," she said, "the spirits sent him healing knowledge in dream visions, such as the right prayer to say, an herbal bath recipe, or incense for spiritual practices."

Panti had taught her "about the spirits living within the Indigenous rainforest plants, in the roots, fruits, leaves, bark, and branches. He believed we must thank these spirits for healing all ills and calamities." Word of the spirits' healing powers drove the sick to Panti's hut every day.

These spirits are all around us, Panti had taught; we don't see them as people with bodies but can only see or feel their presence. And the spirits long to help us with everything if we only ask. They answer prayers, heal the sick, and hold our hands when we die.

Hold our hands when we die? Could they hold Dad's hands?

"So the spirits heal," I said, needing clarification. "Not you or Panti?"

"Yes. And as far as the spiritual goes, well, that's a whole different kind of invisible."

A different kind of invisible? Different like the invisible inside Barton Creek Cave?

"Do you teach that, too? A *different kind* of invisible?"

She nodded. "You have to learn *that*," she said with emphasis. "You have to understand Maya spiritual healing."

I had to ask her about my dark encounter with—with what, exactly? I tried to describe my experience to her, saying, "I couldn't understand what was happening to me. It felt so strong and intense inside the cave."

She nodded. "Well, that makes sense. Tomorrow will be the Day of the Dead when the veil between the physical and spiritual worlds becomes very thin."

Dr. Ariana's wisdom about the supernatural felt right. She'd acquired her insights after years of cutting through the jungles of our material world. Since Panti's death at the age of one hundred three, Dr. Ariana's success in Maya medicine had led to her books and teachings.

"I have a very public life, and I teach around the world," she said with pride.

"I was wondering," I asked, "what would Don Panti's message be for the world today?"

She sat back, laughing as she quoted the essence of the curandero's philosophy: "Most people think too much. Get them to laugh, and half their trouble and sickness will go away. The blessed herbs will do the rest."

I'll remember that when I feel sad about Dad.

With our time together at an end, I stood up. "Could I ask one more question? What would you recommend for traveler's diarrhea?"

She laughed and said, "Try the tincture of jackass bitters. It's in the shops in town."

Back in San Ignacio, I sought out her herbs and tinctures to bring home. A few days later, a bout of traveler's diarrhea hit me, but the jackass bitters knocked it out frighteningly fast.

30

HIS FIRST VISIT

Two months after returning from Belize, a calamity pushed me onto an emotional journey of scrubbing through a private jungle of pain, tearing at its thorny vines, and slipping down grief's muddy slopes. A hollow ache within offered no hope of relief.

During the Christmas holidays, Dad walked two feet from the kitchen table to a counter, faltered, and said, "I just can't catch my breath."

His damaged diaphragm couldn't provide him with enough oxygen, so his heart was giving out. Dad was sinking fast.

After that sad sight, needing solace, I stepped outside onto Mom and Dad's back deck into the fresh, cool December air. I remembered Dr. Ariana sharing Panti's healing words and opened my phone to listen to our recorded interview. Settling in a deck chair, I heard the chachalaca birds chatter as Dr. Ariana talked about the healing power of laughter. *Don't think too much. Laugh, and half your troubles and sickness will go away. Learn that there's a whole different kind of invisible.*

I looked up at the sky and the cold fog rolling over the Marin

Headlands. Dad was dying. What kind of invisible awaited him? I shivered and returned inside to sit beside my father.

On a Saturday in January, Rob and I found ourselves on a frantic drive from Southern California to Marin General Hospital, the hum of the tires on the highway hardly drowning out my fears. The winter sky hung heavy with gray, mirroring the weight on my chest.

After Dad had been rushed to Emergency with a severe respiratory infection, he was placed in the ICU. During our eight-hour drive, I shifted on the cold leather car seat as my thoughts ricocheted between hope and dread.

At the hospital, we searched for my father, running down sterile, fluorescent-lit hallways; we found him amid beeps of monitors, whispered voices, and shuffling footsteps. In a glassed-in ICU room, family and friends had gathered around a doctor. It was a sad montage of love and despair. My heart sank as the doctor's clinical and unyielding words cut through the air; the machines surrounding Dad futilely tethered him to life.

Death was spiriting my father away.

We all stood silent after the physician left. A quiet nurse moved with precision, disconnecting the web of IV tubes and monitors before she transferred Dad to a private room where we'd await his death. A somber procession, his wife, daughters, sons, in-laws, grandchildren, and lifelong friends, walked down long, echoing hallways to a new room. Heavy with sorrow, we drew around his bed, as he would have loved, circling him with devotion, much like the times we once shared in Orvieto. For him, this created the perfect farewell.

I took my place beside him, holding his frail hand, its warmth fading yet familiar. For five hours, from three o'clock until eight, I sat stiff and silent in an unforgiving plastic chair. Helpless, I watched Dad slip further away as his breathing slowed. The only comfort I could offer was the simple act of massaging his hand with lotion, my fingers working gently over his skin, now pale and paper-thin. The lotion's faint scent mingled with the sterile hospital air during my fragile attempt to soothe him.

As tears swam in my eyes, I focused on this small act, willing it to mean something, to ease his journey. I whispered, my voice cracking, "Does that feel okay, Dad?"

He answered with a raspy breath, a single, soft word: "Yes." It was his last.

An unbearable silence followed, as though the world itself held its breath. I clung to Dad's hand, knowing that when I let go, I'd be letting go of him forever.

As the hours passed, my thoughts flew back to a long-ago memory.

On my way to UC Davis, the twenty-year-old me had humped my luggage angrily downstairs to our driveway. I had left Mom standing over a pile of Italian clothes from my year abroad after a big blow-up over what to pack. She said I had to bring my black leather Italian trench coat. I said wearing it in Davis would make me look like an SS officer.

Saying nothing, Dad followed me outside after grabbing more bags.

He stood by, waiting to say goodbye, as I slammed the trunk of the car. "You know," he said, "when you were a baby, and we first moved to San Francisco, your mother and her family gave me such a hard time about moving so far from Ohio. And I couldn't take it anymore."

Listening, I spied rare tears swimming in his eyes.

"One night," he said, his voice softly breaking, "it got so bad I thought about leaving. But all I had to do was look at you, and I just couldn't. I couldn't leave you."

An overwhelming wave of his love ran through me. I realized for the first time that, as his first baby daughter, I had ushered him into his new life as a father.

After a last hug, he sent me off with his frequent advice on working hard. "Okay, head down, ass up!"

I drove off, blinking back my tears, awash in Dad's calming love.

Now, under harsh fluorescent hospital lights, I would've given anything to stand on that driveway again and tell him how much I loved him.

We all took turns kissing him goodbye. To hug and kiss him one last time, Mom leaned toward him, weeping, five months shy of their sixtieth anniversary.

His breaths grew farther and farther apart.

I traded looks with my sister-in-law Charlotte, her eyes shining with tears of pain. She had grown up in New Orleans; Dad affectionately called her "Short'nin' Bread." As a critical care nurse, she was well-versed in the ways of the dying.

After we timed three long minutes between each gulp of breath, she whispered to me so the others couldn't hear: "Lenore, tell him he can go. Sometimes, they hang on because of us."

The room swirled. *I can't do that.*

My body felt immensely heavy as I struggled off my plastic chair to bend close to his ear.

"It's okay to go," I said, choking on my words. "We all love you, and you were a good Papa, and we'll be all right."

He lifted his chin, took two gulps of air, and then nothing. A cold finality sunk deep into my chest as hot tears rolled down my face. *He's really gone now, forever.*

Unable to move and still holding his hand, I stayed behind as everyone peeled out of his room. I ached to tell him once more how much I adored him. A nurse came in; it was time for me to leave. I kissed his forehead and whispered into his ear, "Goodbye, Dad. I will love you forever."

Outside his room, I found Rob leaning against a wall.

"He's gone." I crumpled into his arms.

The Saturday after Dad's death, during my sleepless night ensconced in Rob's arms in an unforgiving darkness, I silently pondered if Dad was okay and at peace. He should've been—he'd spent enough hours on his knees in Mass.

I wondered aloud, "What happens when you die? Is Dad okay where he is?" A sad sigh escaped me. "At least we were lucky to be with him when he died."

"I will never forget it. To be there with him was the most amazing experience in my life," said Rob. "Except for the birth of our babies."

I snuggled closer to him for warmth. "Yes, amazing. I hope he's happy now and free of pain."

"Of course, he is."

"But how will I know? I mean, there's no proof that he is. I can't Google it or check with him on the phone."

"No, no, but I'm sure he is."

"I guess we'll never know what happened when he died," I said, sinking under the covers. I hated this insidious loss and this new, unwanted life without Dad. A painful sorrow grabbed hold of me in the darkness; I couldn't fathom living without Dad in my life, but I had no choice but to endure it.

The next morning, after a somber breakfast, my siblings and I convened in Mom and Dad's bedroom with the door closed. Shell-shocked and numb, holding pens and pads, we organized our tasks for a burial and a memorial Mass during the coming week.

We planned his burial and an after-party at Dad's house for Wednesday. On Thursday, we'd hold his memorial Mass for four hundred people and then feed them all (we were Italian, after all). After that, his closest loved ones and out-of-towners would gather for another after-party back at the house with catered Italian food and lots of booze. We listed our tasks: the cemetery, the priest, the singer for the Mass, the military honor guard for his burial, the restaurant, and the caterer. We'd spend as much money in only four days as we would've for a wedding. Four of the five of us had our areas of expertise: the banker, the accountant, the lawyer, and me.

"Lenore will write the obituary and eulogy," said Ricci.

After our meeting, we walked into a disruptive din of phone calls, doorbells, flower deliveries, and visitors inundating our house. Leo turned to me and said, "I feel like I'm having an out-of-body experience."

"God, yes!" I replied. I stepped into Dad's office, saying, "Now, I've got to get to work." I locked the door and sat at his desk in the quiet, facing his computer to do the unimaginable: weave together the threads of his full life.

To start, I began listing his charities. But the list was endless. *Jesus, so many charities.*

I stopped and put my head in my hands. Distracted, I rummaged through his desk, discovering his file for my wedding, packed with ephemera, guest lists, florist bills, and wedding expenses.

Then, a paper fluttered to the floor. I picked up Dad's list of every country he had explored, all forty-eight, from Oman to Sweden to Argentina to China.

China. Tiananmen Square. Good God, Mom and Dad had gotten out just in time.

But not before Dad took snapshots of Mom smiling and posing with protesters against a backdrop of their red banners demanding democracy. Now, at the end of his full life, I sat alone in his office in tears, holding his faded list of countries.

In a file drawer, I spotted two fat legal-size file folders, marked in his hand as "Lenore's Articles" and "Lenore's Writing." I found every published piece I'd sent him, dating from my college years until now—newspaper and magazine clippings, online articles, and my guidebook work, everything. *He must've been proud of his travel-writer daughter.*

Returning the files to his desk drawer, I fumbled the thickest one, and two items fell onto the desktop, a hospital baby bracelet and a pair of TWA junior-pilot wings. The tiny bracelet spelled our last name, A-S-I-A-N-O,

Dad's snapshot of Mom in Tiananmen Square with student protesters before the tanks rolled in.
Image courtesy of the author's collection.

in pink and white beads. Was this put on my wrist in the hospital after I was born?

The golden metal pilot wings glinted in the sunlight pouring from his office window. During the Jet Age, stewardesses, as they were called, led children into the cockpit where the pilot presented them with pilot's wings. Holding these mementos in my hand, I marveled at how Dad had kept them all these years for me to find.

I dissolved into tears, slipping into a bottomless, oily pool of darkness. I couldn't believe he was gone. I picked up my phone and texted Grace, who was out shopping before the coming onslaught.

"Don't forget the Patrón," I said. "The big bottle!"

I settled myself in front of Dad's computer screen. He'd never talked about his accomplishments. How would I capture his essence?

My fingers raced over the keyboard. "Born in the hard-scrabble steel town of Steubenville, Ohio, the son of Italian immigrants, Leonard Asiano took his blows and overcame his obstacles. Like a sailor on heavy seas, he plotted his escape from Cleveland as a young man. After an Army hitch, he graduated from the University of San Francisco and got accepted into the US Navy's Officer Candidate School. Then, he circumnavigated the globe."

I put my head in my hands. *Damn it. This doesn't work.*

Then, I remembered when Dad's oldest friend Morey had told a story about an important course correction Dad had taken in eighth grade.

A couple of years ago, Rob and I visited with Morey at a San Diego seaside restaurant. On a cross-country driving trip, Morey had just come from San Francisco after visiting Mom and Dad before heading back to Cleveland.

"I've always loved your family," Morey said over drinks. "And your dad. He did a good job with you guys." He leaned toward us. "Did he ever tell you about Miss Lichty?"

"No," I said. "He doesn't talk much about himself."

"Oh, you'll love this," said Morey, his eyes smiling. "She was our eighth-grade counselor. And your dad got so mad at her before we graduated because she put him on the industrial track at Cleveland Heights High. She did that with all the Italian boys. So he went and told her that he wanted the college prep track, but she fought him, saying, 'Why do you want the college prep track? Italian kids never go to college.' Your dad got so mad. Your grandparents had to go down and straighten her out. And guess what? He got on the college prep track."

Morey sat back in his chair, grinning. "And he did really well, all straight As!"

Remembering that moment, I began writing anew, confident about capturing Dad.

During a writing break, I found an email printout someone had left on his desk from a member of the Krewe of Thoth. Ah, yes, Dad's men's club in New Orleans, famous for its afternoon children's parade during Mardi Gras. More importantly, they supported charities for the homeless and the sick. Every Sunday before Fat Tuesday, Dad and my brother Ricci, donned masks and costumes and joined hundreds of fellow members to ride aboard Thoth's floats during the Children's Hospital kids' parade.

"He really enjoyed Thoth," Ricci had told me once. "He loved passing toys to the sick kids lining the streets in wheelchairs."

As the little kids yelled, "Hey, Mista, throw me somethin'!" Thoth threw heavy, meaning they never skimped on the toys, stuffed animals, candy, and revered golden coins they tossed. That compassionate approach matched Dad's values. "He loved how they 'threw heavy,'" said Ricci.

The email printout was from a fellow Thoth member:

> I was so fortunate to meet Mr. Leonard while riding together in the Mardi Gras parade. What a special person and such a role model for those lucky enough to cross his path.

At their next Mardi Gras parade, Thoth would honor our father with a memorial sign hung on their lead float:

Hail Thoth!

In Memory

Fellow Thoth Rider and Gentleman

Leonard C. Asiano

Six days after Dad died, as Rob and I prepared to drive home, my oldest friend Martea invited me to decompress at her country home for a few days.

Grieving my father's death on horseback at Martea's country place.
© Lenore Greiner 2013.

This was a comfort since Rob had to get back to work and I had no idea how to return to my old life.

Martea and I had become friends as toddlers when our moms became best friends. Our families were pisano, family members not related by blood but by love. Outr parents were connected to each other forever as godparents to our respective siblings.

On the first morning of my stay, a firm tug of my left big toe woke me up.

Bleary with sleep, I thought, *That's weird. I'm alone, but that tug felt so real.*

In the breaking dawn's strange penumbra of shadow and light, I roused myself from sleep, slowly understanding that someone, something, wanted me to awaken. I lay in Martea's guest room in a big bed surrounded by French antiques in California's Gold Country, near where the first spark of gold was discovered in 1849.

I realized that, yes, it was Dad, it must've been Dad. His presence filled the entire room.

Feeling Dad's unmistakable, intense presence, I sailed on a profound sense of knowing, a knowing truer than I'd ever felt. Just like when that voice of Jesus sounded in my mind in the empty church when Rob underwent surgery.

Messages came as feelings, not words, embodied upon waves of peace, an unbearably rich emotion washing through me.

"I'm all right," the voice whispered. *Dad.*

Warm tears filled my eyes as he answered what I had been silently asking during the crush and chaos after his death.

"I'm at peace," he said.

I've got to write this down, I thought—yet I stayed motionless. If I moved, my intense serenity might break away.

"I'm okay. Jeez, that was something else," he said of his passing. "I am here."

He said that his deceased brother and his parents had greeted him, standing beside his grandmother, whom he called "Nono."

"I'm not quite moving into it yet, and they're helping me."

I knew this meant he existed in a transitional state.

Then Dad said, "You must meditate more."

I smiled. *The parenting never ends.*

Then, Dad faded away.

Gone. He was gone.

He left me in the quiet room, suspended in a radiant stillness. A profound peace engulfed my soul as if his departure carried off the weight of all my suffering over the past week.

An aching realness and a tenderness lingered, filling the space where despair might have taken root. *That was more than a memory—that was his presence, unmistakable and alive.*

The vividness of it left me breathless, as did the reassurance he radiated: a quiet certainty that he was at peace, wrapped in a joy so boundless that the boundaries of life and death felt irrelevant.

For the first time, I knew I could free myself of the fearful notions that had haunted me: hellfire from Catholic sermons and whispers from a shadowy Mayan underworld, all pale imitations of the reality I now sensed. Dad wasn't lost in darkness; he lived in light. His joy transcended comprehension, and for a moment, it enveloped me too.

The revelation was seismic. Life, with all its suffering, suddenly felt like a transient test, a passage leading to something infinitely greater. In that moment, I glimpsed a possibility that our pain, our fears, our struggles might be rendered insignificant by what lay beyond. *Are we never truly alone? Are we shepherded by unseen hands—angels, ancestors, or forces unnamed—until we arrive in a place of radiant peace?* If so, perhaps that place makes every burden, every wound, not only endurable but meaningful.

I clung to this thinking, desperate to hold on to the warmth Dad left behind. It wasn't just my memory of him—it was him, a parting gift from a father to his daughter. I could almost hear his voice saying, *Don't worry. It's all as it should be.*

Driven to preserve this moment, I left my bed and reached for my journal. Words spilled out in a torrent as I tried to capture everything: the peace, the warmth, the love.

Later, I pulled back the heavy curtains at my window. Outside, the world gleamed, bathed in gold. Martea's horses stood motionless in their white-fenced paddock, their breath visible in the cold morning light. Behind ancient oaks, a rising sun gilded the grass and trees in a way that felt almost holy.

I smiled.

In that moment, I understood: Grief and joy are not opposites but threads of the same tapestry, woven together to form something profound, something eternal that makes earthly suffering insignificant. There was something bigger at play here. Dad was here—not in a distant realm but close, tangible, like the warmth of the sun or the glint of the pasture. His love, his essence, remained as a gift to carry forward.

For the first time since Dad had died, I felt peaceful and accepting. Would my feelings last? Or would that ugly world without Dad bombard me again? How long could I stand living in it? Confronting my earthly suffering yet feeling pleased about Dad's happiness in the afterlife made me feel crazy.

I padded downstairs, following the aroma of coffee—Martea was already up, mug in hand, wishing me a good morning with a soft smile.

I sat across from her, cupping my cold hands around my hot coffee cup. "Something happened this morning," I began, my voice barely above a whisper. "Dad came to me. He wanted me to know that he's okay. I've been wondering all week, and now . . ." I trailed off, the words catching in my throat.

Martea's gaze didn't waver. "Of course," she said gently, her voice steady with belief.

I glanced at her, grateful for her lack of skepticism. "He hasn't left, Martea. He's here—around me."

"Oh, absolutely."

I took a deep breath, the memory of his Mass still vivid. "You know, sitting in the front pew, I felt so exposed, so raw. I kept hoping my eulogy did him justice. Then, as I looked at his portrait on the altar, something happened." I paused, running a finger along the rim of my cup. "His face— it wasn't just a picture. It glowed with life. His smile, his eyes ... they shimmered, like he was looking right at me. We connected. And then I glanced away for just a second."

Martea leaned in.

"And when I looked back," I continued, my voice trembling slightly, "it was just a photograph on an easel. But that moment—it stayed with me. The glow, the warmth, the peace I felt ... it was real. And I *knew*. He was happy. Hell, he was even enjoying it."

Martea chuckled; she knew Dad's joie de vivre well. "He loves you, you know that?"

I nodded, tears brimming in my eyes. "Yeah, I do. I just wish I knew what to make of it all."

"You don't have to, Lenore," she said, her voice calm. "Just accept it— like you accept his love."

I sat back, letting her words settle. Martea was right. Dad's love didn't need logic or proof; it just was. The now brighter morning light caught my coffee cup, glinting off the rim like a tiny halo.

I smiled to myself. *Maybe Dad didn't really leave after all. Maybe he never will.*

For the first time in days, I eased into a subtle tranquility. And that was good enough for now.

31

A WRITER ALWAYS NEEDS FEEDBACK

The morning after I flew home from Martea's, I unpacked my suitcase, including the two treasures that had fallen from Dad's clippings file: a tiny baby bracelet and a pair of golden TWA junior pilot's wings. Their weight in my hand felt both physical and emotional, standing for Dad's love and my history.

The baby bracelet, a delicate strand of pink-and-white beads spelling out my maiden name, had circled my wrist from the moment I entered the world—a fragile symbol of belonging. Dad must have been overjoyed on that gloomy winter morning in a gray Midwestern city, welcoming his first child at four a.m. I imagined him rushing from the fathers' waiting room to the nursery, his heart swelling with love as he caught his first glimpse of my tiny face.

Another scene shimmered in my mind: Dad fumbling with dimes at the payphone to call and share his news, his voice thick with emotion. Not just a trinket—my baby bracelet was his first gift, imbued with his love, each bead strung with hope, each letter a quiet declaration: She is mine, and I am hers.

Now, it was as if I held a fragment of his love, undiminished over the years. A talisman of the first love that ushered me into the world, the bracelet whispered to me of our bond that began in my first moments and, like the bracelet itself, was small but enduring. I tucked it into my jewelry box.

I studied my golden pilot's wings as their metallic sheen caught the morning sun streaming through my bedroom window. They weren't just a keepsake—they symbolized Dad's other gifts to me: my wanderlust, my yearning for adventure, my instinct to take flight in every sense of the word. He had always encouraged me to embrace the world and soar beyond the boundaries of the familiar. My golden wings represented his quiet permission to take off and discover the world, confident that I'd always wing my way home.

I placed my golden wings in my jewelry box next to my baby bracelet. Both items were more precious than gold, both anchors and guideposts connecting me to my father. Closing the lid, I felt the faintest flicker of hope and the courage to embrace what lay ahead, no matter how uncertain. Over the past week, I'd worried that, as life continued at home, I'd leave Dad behind, forgotten, as if betraying him. But I'd never betray him; every step I'd take would be woven with his love.

And with this knowledge, I also understood that even loss can lead somewhere beautiful and meaningful.

On a tranquil Sunday morning, almost a month after the memorial, I crawled out of bed before dawn, sleepless, and left Rob asleep.

Downstairs, I sipped coffee and read on the living room couch until

I sensed a familiar presence moving near the front door. I glanced up yet saw no one in the dim light. *Oh, Rob's up,* I thought. *He must've stepped into the guest bath.*

A few minutes later, I looked up again, thinking I'd see him near the front door. But then I heard him snoring upstairs.

Suddenly, the air in the room became charged with an unseen presence. It was my dad. I knew it.

Wishing to hear him again, I settled into a meditative stillness, eyes closed, heart open. All at once, I felt his love—warm and encircling, like a familiar embrace. *Dad.*

I placed my pen on paper and wrote a word that came to me—then another and another, never knowing the next. "Mom's okay—I watch her." I was transcribing words I felt, Dad's words.

Dad also had thoughts about his kids and grandchildren. His words came—gently, steadily, and marked with wisdom and warmth. At first, I got fragments, or thoughts, and feelings entwined, but soon, sentences flowed in, one after another, because I *knew* his spirit was beside me.

I scribbled everything down quickly until Dad took a long pause.

When I stopped to read, I shook my head, astounded. *This can't be real. Am I really listening to Dad? Or is my grief making the fantastical real?*

No, he'd spoke directly into my heart just like at Martea's.

All this time, I'd been worried about how hard it was for him to leave us all.

But, as if in response to my concerns, he said, "It's worth staying here."

Wow, heaven must be wonderful.

Then I heard, "Heaven *is* wonderful; it's sound and light and indescribable. It's love."

I breathed deeply, listening for more.

"Get right spiritually. Pursue it. Love it. The right path, the way. They're all understanding this now." He was referring to Mom and my siblings. "They're each working through things, and they'll be all right—that's why I went first, to teach. There is peace. Know it, and it will come. Just be. I am. Believe it all."

I choked on unshed tears as my pen traveled across my page.

He gave me messages for my siblings and Mom: "Reach out to Leo—tell him I'm very proud of all he's done. He's the brightest, and we had a special relationship. Tell Grace she's not alone—she feels alone. Tell your mother she's being selfish. She needs to let go of me. Tell her to think about that in church.

"Don't take on all their troubles. Let it happen. Yes, you are the oldest kid, but don't do their work for them."

Afterward, I paced around my living room. *Do I share those messages? If I did, nobody would believe me.* I could just say I had dreamed about Dad.

Dad found it surprising we could communicate, and he predicted I would travel a lot. *Well, that's good since I'm a travel writer.*

Dad paused again. Tears welled in my eyes as I told him how much I missed him and that I was trying to be strong.

"Just be." He knew.

I wanted to know if my eulogy had made him proud. *A writer always needs feedback.*

"Extremely. I was there. Remember when you looked at my picture and you saw my emotion?"

After jotting down his question, I wrote, "Yes, I will never forget the moment your altar portrait came alive. I saw happiness and love."

"That's it, kid. That's all you need."

He started drifting away. "Gotta go."

"Please come back," I wrote. Dad was gone, but he was never truly absent.

In the silence, I closed my journal, went upstairs, and waited for Rob to awaken. As with Martea, I knew I could tell him about what had just happened in our living room, and Rob would believe me. And that filled me with an ethereal sense of calm.

I believed Dad's presence would lessen my agony. Yet as spiritually and peacefully as I wished to live, despite these pleasant afterlife encounters, I couldn't avoid a gut-wrenching mourning period.

My days began calmly as I spent mornings alone to meditate and journal. But when a word, a song, or a memory reminded me of Dad, grief tore me apart and forced me to endure the raging storms within.

I learned the hard way that there are no shortcuts around grief. I couldn't bypass its power nor avoid the slow, painful work of pushing through its turbulence one moment at a time.

Why was this so painful? Because Dad was my biggest supporter. The one who loved to share my published clippings with anyone who came over to his house. The one who *listened* to me, who stood by me for too many hours in too many surgical waiting rooms.

One evening I stood in our living room, my body quaking with rage over Rob's ever-growing piles of unread aviation and guitar magazines. I screamed, "Please! I am begging you, for the love of God, will you please recycle those goddamn magazines."

Seeing his face, I remembered how much I'd unleashed my hostility at him the day before, after he'd asked a simple question. "No, you cannot ask me to do the dishes," I said after lying around all afternoon. "My dad just died."

I'd been making my anger a habit. "Nope," I said another time. "I didn't get groceries today. I just lost my father, so I don't have to."

Rob wasn't my only victim. I knew that anyone who said a wrong word risked getting bitch-slapped across town and back. I careened around in my car, honking at the faintest slight. I barked at hapless salespeople who didn't answer me fast enough, and I hung up on my bank's stupid customer service rep. I grimaced at the elderly man standing in front of me in a grocery line, thinking, *Why is he alive and Dad isn't?*

Each evening, I trudged upstairs to fall into our bed, exhausted, thinking, *I can't live like this.*

One morning, I forced myself out of bed to call the local hospice and dragged my sorry self in for grief counseling. I remembered how much I loved talking with Martea, how her believing me made me feel at ease. And I loved how Rob listened to me as I read Dad's words from my journal. I had to veer onto a new path, the path of healing.

In her small office, I met Kate for our first counseling session. I believed she had the saddest, most formidable job around, and I even half-smiled at her in pity.

We hit it off at once, sharing the same sense of humor and appreciation for yoga, meditation, and living a spiritual life. She thought nothing of slipping off her chair, throwing her legs up the wall in a helpful inverted yoga pose, then twisting around to the floor and hopping back into her chair.

And we laughed—a lot.

She taught me about the bereavement process.

"So how long does it last?" I asked.

"Well, you'll always feel sadness but right now you're in the thick of the newness and rawness of grieving. For how long really depends on the person."

"Because everyone grieves in their own way?"

"Yes, and what you're doing, keeping a journal, writing down your feelings, dreams, memories will help you."

Fidgeting, I opened up about the day Dad died as Kate patiently listened despite hearing variations of the same story.

I downloaded my trauma in catharsis. "You see," I said, "his house was too dangerous for him to live in. He'd tell us kids, 'No way! I'm leaving this house feet first!' Then he got so weak from a cough that the paramedics did carry him out feet first. That's when I got serious calls from my family, telling me to get there fast.

"First, I heard 'He's in Emergency, and they're keeping him overnight.' Then, 'He crashed, and now he's on a breathing tube.'"

I paused, the writer in me thinking how "crashed," medical slang for a stopped heart, was also the right word to describe life crashing to a stop. "Then," I continued, "he crashed again, and was in ICU."

"So, it was happening quickly," said Kate.

"Yeah. I ordered Rob to come home, but he didn't believe that it was that bad. I remember jerking luggage down like a robot. When he saw my good black clothes inside his suitcase, he asked, 'What's this? We don't need any funeral clothes.' So casually. And I just froze. I walked past him into the bathroom in silence. That's when he knew it was serious. I wasn't talking."

I found myself wringing my hands. "When we got there, I held his hand for five hours."

Suddenly, I remembered what Dr. Ariana had said about how loving spirits will hold our hands as we lie dying. *Was that why I'd been able to sit there, steady, holding Dad's hand for hours? Were loving spirits holding us both, carrying us through?*

Kate waited for me to continue.

"Oh, I was just . . . remembering something," I said, hesitating. But then I decided to trust her with my private thoughts. She knew grief; maybe she'd understand my glimpses of the afterlife through my father's words.

"Well, many things come in during meditation," she answered.

How would she know this for sure?

Leaving her office after making my next appointment, I promised myself to stay centered while wading through melancholy's strong wake.

Every Sunday, I began to take care of myself by heading alone to a seaside meditation garden to pray, meditate, and journal, serenaded by the music of the sea. In those soothing moments, I went easy on myself—it takes a long time to heal. Bit by bit, my rage lessened as did grief's sharp bite on my heart.

One night as Rob and I lay in bed, I felt the unmistakable touch of Dad's hand upon my shoulder as if to remind me all was well. I absorbed the very real feel of his hand as tears sprang into my eyes; Dad was reaching out to me from beyond death and into the material world.

"Dad's here, honey," I said softly to Rob. "His hand is right on my shoulder."

"Oh, that's wonderful. He loves you, you know."

"Do you ever feel him, too?"

"No, but I know he's around."

I turned off the light and snuggled deeper in bed, content. I accepted Dad's strong presence, not as a cruel delusion, but as a different kind of invisible, as Dr. Ariana had taught. These experiences, a hand on my shoulder or his voice in my heart, confirmed other worlds exist, spiritual realms.

That was no coincidence, meeting Dr. Ariana only two and a half months before Dad died. Since she lived in the world of spirits, she believed that a spirit screamed at me in Barton Creek Cave during my very rough initiation into invisible realms. Afterward, I found the courage to tap into that different kind of invisible and keep listening to Dad. As time passed, I began to love the moments when his favorite sayings surfaced in my thoughts, perfectly timed to whisper into my ear as if the universe conspired to keep his voice alive.

I'd only wanted to know if he was okay. Instead, I'd received a precious and profound connection with him; his presence, though unseen, assured me the boundaries between life and death, between the tangible and intangible, dissolved in his comforting embrace and defied explanation.

My father's presence seemed woven into the air. This kind of invisible never left a void; it always felt certain and unshakable, like a beautiful truth that wouldn't let me go.

32

MY FATHER'S MOON

As much as I tried to remain in that place of calm, the anguish of my grieving returned, again and again, evolving into the physical as a cruel pain stabbing me in the back between my shoulder blades.

Seeing me whine after another sharp, sudden twinge, Rob asked, "What's wrong?"

"It's this random pain. Don't know why." I twisted my tense shoulders. "It comes and goes. Nothing I do stops it, and it's getting worse."

I sought treatment from the capable Dr. Anika, an Indian Ayurvedic medical doctor. In her office, draped with sari fabric, she took one look at me.

"It's a heart chakra issue—a broken heart."

"Oh, my dad just died," I said nonchalantly.

She had me lie face down on her massage table as she lowered the lights, lit incense, and filled the room with a slow, melodic Sanskrit chant for a father who had just died. Her hands expertly prepared a warm, medicinal oil infused with herbs for a daughter grieving her father. She dug in with strong fingers after running ribbons of warm oil up and down my spine. A tight, pained breath escaped me.

"You're full of knots." As she spoke, a chill breeze slipped over my bare legs. Then, that similar rush of peace cascaded over me.

Dad.

I felt his presence just beyond my shoulder. Recognizing this familiar wave of emotion from my meditations, I surrendered to its intensity and accepted his gift. The darkened room seemed to expand to contain the immensity of his love. The scent of the incense grew stronger, and the sacred music seemed to vibrate. My breath calmed.

"Oh, there's a presence here," said Dr. Anika.

She feels him, too. "My dad. He comes to me sometimes."

I couldn't bring myself to share how, since his death, I'd heard his voice during meditation. But soon, my knots released, and the mysterious stabbing pain faded away.

As her fingers circled over my loosened muscles, she said, "Hmm, you're like a baby now. Thank him for his help."

Then I heard my dad say, "Just doing my job." It had been his common saying to us kids after we'd thanked him for something.

"Oh," said Dr. Anika, "now he's saying he'll love you forever."

What? I shook with shock; tears sprang into my eyes. "That's exactly what I whispered into his ear before leaving his hospital room," I choked. "On the night he died."

Her validation of Dad's presence was a profound gift. Knowing she heard him too sent a flood of relief through my body. Quicksilver-fast messages rushed in. *Don't dwell on his death, his illness, with such deep mourning,* I told myself. *Dwell upon the great things he did. Dwell upon your own family and your happy future.*

"Then, at your funeral," I heard him say, "your loved ones will feel love and joy for you."

"How long has it been since your father died?" asked Dr. Anika.

"He died on January 12th."

As I wiped away tears on the sheet, she pointed to a calendar.

"Today is February 14th. Exactly one month. You can do a puja for him, a special ritual to pray for his peace. Do this up to forty-five days after his passing to help with his transition."

Apparently, it took time for the dead to get used to being dead.

During a trip to India, I had experienced pujas, sacred rites redolent of incense, tiny flames, abundant flowers, tinkling bells, and drapes of resplendent silk. Dr. Anika's idea resonated deeply since pujas always created an intense peace and closeness to God.

Both Rob and I had fought boredom during the Masses of our childhoods, reciting rote chants and prayers. As adults, we abandoned Catholicism's black-and-white dogma. After learning in India that all paths lead to God, I drew closer to Eastern practices, the simplicity of Buddhism's mindful meditation, and the intensity of Hinduism's devotion to God.

"You know, my dad always said that India was his favorite trip. We both loved it there."

"Ah, the forty-third day after his death will be very auspicious. A full moon will rise in the evening, and that day commemorates Saraswati, the goddess of knowledge, music, and the arts."

"Perfect. My dad was a musician, and I'm a writer."

"Pray for him, and let his good karma become tenfold to help him through his transition. And do charity on his behalf."

"Yes, I've donated to the hospice where I'm getting grief counseling."

On the forty-third day after Dad's passing, I dressed in my finest Indian silks and entered a Hindu temple. Rob and our son Hunter agreed to join me. They suffered, too. Perhaps this would help them. Kamal, a Hindu priest in his thirties, greeted us, wearing a warm smile and pure white Indian clothes. He asked us to wash our hands and sit cross-legged on a carpet on the white marble floor. A pantheon of Hindu deities stood over us, each inside their own marble niche, arrayed in floral garlands, lavish silks, and gold tinsel. At their feet, offering baskets overflowed.

I gave Kamal a framed photo of Dad smiling. He placed it with great respect upon a brass tray laden with marigolds and roses, incense, holy water, coconut, rice, crimson powder, a lit oil lamp, and a plate of Indian sweets. My body relaxed as our resplendent puja began.

"Now, we will honor your father," said Kamal in a soft voice. Overseen by the gods, he gently chanted in Sanskrit while purifying us with wafts of incense and sprinklings of holy water. Then he waved a tray of tiny oil lamp flames around our heads. A stillness crept in, followed by a sense of unfolding love, like a pink cloud expanding above our heads.

"Let's chant the sacred mantra, Shanti Om, for peace, for our peace, and for his peace." He placed a tilak, a crimson powder mark, between our eyebrows.

"For concentration."

He even placed a tilak on Dad's forehead, and I liked to think he liked that. Kamal placed a marigold on my palm, asking me to chant *Shanti Om*. After Rob and Hunter did the same, he put our flowers on Dad's tray.

Following Dr. Anika's instruction, I prayed "to let his good karma become tenfold to get him through his transition." I gazed over to Dad's picture and found his face aglow as if backlit, giving him life.

He's here with us. He's happy. I floated in gratitude.

An intense calm engulfed my body, and my spine tingled. I turned to Rob and Hunter, finding their faces incandescent with peace.

Concluding the puja, Kamal waved a tray of dancing flames around my father, symbolizing how God drives away the darkness. My throat caught a sob. When we stood up, Kamal shared the Indian sweets as a prasad, or gift, from God. I presented my dakshina, a temple offering of money, and I shot a photo of Dad smiling from his overflowing tray.

As we left the temple, the full moon's huge face hung in the sky like a giant theatrical backdrop.

"It's my father's moon!" I said.

The moon observed us, silent and knowing, as a celestial witness to Dad's peace. Its fullness seemed to embrace Dad's essence, reflecting his tenderness and strength now etched into the night.

Radiating from the heavens, the rising moon whispered to me like a parting gift from my father, a luminous reminder that love endures beyond the veil. With moonlight upon my face, we walked toward our car.

The next morning, my father's voice resonated within me, true and real. Expanding gusts of overwhelming love poured into my body, bringing in more tears, as if my father were wrapping his arms around me to lift me out of despair.

The first thing I heard was "Honor your father and your mother." He knew the puja was in his honor.

"I'm over the moon—yes, I'm smiling," he added, reinforcing my belief that the previous night's moon was his moon.

In the moment, I relived the puja's moments of transcendence. But I had a burning question for him: "What's the afterlife like, Dad?"

"It feels so good to be here, getting used to it. I'm very peaceful and understand so much now. There is so much love."

Then, I asked an even bigger question: "What's death really like?"

"It's like the ending of one movement and the beginning of another." He likened death to that moment of silence between symphony movements, such as when a fast allegro tempo concludes and there's a pause allowing the music to shift seamlessly into a new tempo. In the same way, his death felt effortless, not as an ending but as a brief, quiet transformation freeing my father from his earthly suffering.

I quickly scratched his words into my journal. Then, I put down my pen, savoring his presence, and I felt another truth hang in the air: There is no death, only the beginning of a new life.

33

ONE DREAM AND TWO WINGS

One night, I dreamed about meeting a character from the Wes Anderson film *The Darjeeling Express*. Anderson's wildly creative story follows three brothers who travel to India while processing their father's death. In my dream, one brother joined me on a shopping spree in a fashionable Indian shop.

As if dipping into a rich hippie's closet, we sorted through jumbles of orange-and-red velvet clothing, bright feathered things, long, opulent coats, and high heels. Everything fit me. Then, we found more shops offering even more colorful, lavish arrays of goods.

I woke up.

As I recorded my dream, confusion reigned over its meaning. So I wrote down some questions. Was it something to do with taking a creative path going forward? To blossom more as an artist, display my brilliant colors, and relish future multi-colored successes? Was I holding myself

Draping myself in beads as a three-year-old creative.
Image courtesy of the author's collection.

back, career-wise, despite recently authoring a guidebook? In my father's eyes, I was an excellent writer and a screaming success. Why couldn't I see myself that way?

Working in my office later, creativity poured through me as I composed personal travel stories and essays. By the end of the day, imbued with satisfaction after a good day of writing, I felt creative and artistic. Maybe my dream had bestowed some magic and inspiration.

I shut the lid of my laptop and sat back in my chair, driven to sign up for the photography, painting, and writing courses I had kept putting off. A voice kept telling me I lacked the energy—my grieving sucked it all up. This time, I ignored that voice. I opened my laptop and signed up for a travel writers' conference in Marin County that I'd long wanted to attend.

How about applying to get into that travel writing intensive during the conference? For years I'd dreamed about it. I loved the famous travel writer and journalist who would lead it. He was known for his witty, insightful, and adventurous storytelling.

I took a leap of faith and sent off my application with a writing sample.

Maybe I'll wear my TWA junior pilot's wings during the conference. It's time to spread my wings.

34

FROM MILL VALLEY, WITH LOVE

In Marin to attend the travel writers' conference, I felt ecstatic about my acceptance into the travel writing intensive. When it ended that afternoon, our instructor sent our small group off with an assignment—go someplace, sit with a pen and paper, and see what comes up.

In Mill Valley's village, I took a seat on a bench in Bill Graham Plaza on an August afternoon.

While waiting for something to write, I saw the slanting rays of the summer sun through the redwoods and caught the familiar aroma of my childhood rambles in nature. I gazed up the hillsides spilling into the village, thick with cedar, oak, and California laurel trees. Neatly preserved Victorians and modern boxes stood half-hidden in the narrow, steep canyons of Mount Tamalpais, the Sleeping Maiden, with hair tumbling westward to the Pacific Ocean.

Mill Valley had always inspired me. As a young girl, I wrote in my diary about the tiny treasures of simpler times—the thrill of climbing Horse Hill to stroke the horses' soft muzzles and the scent of wild sweet anise lingering on my fingers after gnawing the stalks and chewing on tender miner's lettuce leaves I'd picked along creek beds.

In the past, returning as an adult meant stepping back into the warm embrace of my sprawling Italian family, with Dad, the constant who bridged my childhood and adulthood. He had been the beloved leader of our tribe.

But on that afternoon, everything had changed with my father gone. And my hometown as I knew it was gone, too. The childhood home where we created so many memories was now rented to attorneys from New York. The place that had once felt like a part of me had become unrecognizable—a shadow town, haunted by echoes of the Mill Valley and father I loved.

I missed the sound of his laughter after one of his bad jokes, and I missed his wild stories that made life feel like an adventure. Like the time he tossed a string of rhinestones into my ten-year-old hands after a night in Tahoe's casinos, declaring, "A showgirl threw these at me." It was absurd, magical, and so unmistakably him. He wove joy and mischief into my childhood.

The weight of these losses could have made this journey back to Mill Valley unbearable. I feared that returning might unravel me, pulling me back into grief's undertow. Yet sitting there amid these changes, I found an unexpected calm. I scribbled in my notebook, "I'm not sad. My present reality is."

What would he say to me now?

"Don't let it get to you, Lenore." That's what he'd say.

I won't let it get to me, Dad. I'll remove the debris from my tangled thoughts and concentrate on mourning you. I know that my grief will grow less intense.

There on the red brick plaza, I imagined Mill Valley had written a letter to me. The light brown letter paper carried the earthy scent of musty redwood groves from the needles decaying in the loam. The ink was purple, a nod to my town's bohemian history.

Dear Lenore,

You are a little Catholic schoolgirl in a scratchy wool uniform, the daydreamer gazing out the tall windows of Our Lady of Mount Carmel School, watching wispy fogs curl through the spiny tops of the redwoods on the high ridges.

Down the street, the Sequoia Theatre is showing a James Bond film, *From Russia With Love*, but you can't see it.

During Mass, the priest announces that the Catholic Church condemns the movie and that watching it is a mortal sin.

Every morning, your father fights the traffic across Golden Gate Bridge to the Financial District so you can grow up here. After a long day, he comes home, grabs dinner, and heads out again, saying, "I've got a church meeting." He's helping to build a new church in downtown Mill Valley.

As a kid, you run freely in the hills or catch pollywogs in sloughs fed by the bay. Your mom has no idea where you are until dinnertime.

As a horse-crazy girl with stringy hair, you stand at Horse Hill's barbed wire fence with blades of grass on your outstretched palm, patiently waiting for the pastured horses to lumber slowly downhill. Their velvety muzzles deftly wipe your palm clean.

As a teenager in bell-bottomed jeans, one May evening, you and a boy ascend stairs and hiking paths built by early city fathers to a wood platform above the village. As an indigo twilight fades, a full moon rises, washing your hometown silver. Dark forested ridges, which Kerouac described as a "roaring sea of trees," line the valley, ending at the Richardson Bay mudflats. Beyond, houseboats bob on the tide, the lights of Sausalito climb Wolfback Ridge, and car headlights on Highway 101 zigzag downhill from the Golden Gate Bridge.

You both draw close together against the chill. You are in love for the first time. You will always remember that moment.

At seventeen, after high school graduation, you ascend Kite Hill and write in your journal that it's time to leave Mill Valley.

The wanderlust gene you inherited from your father has tripped. He offers you two choices for your graduation gift—a used car or a trip to Mexico. You choose Mexico, and he understands since he circumnavigated the globe before his twenty-fifth birthday.

When you move away with your new husband, your dad teases you about writing in your college essay, "I'll never leave the shadow of Mount Tam."

Awe-struck, I stood up, lucky to have grown up in a magical place so perfect for a creative child.

Two blocks from the plaza, the Catholic church my dad helped build stood as a testament to his faith. Mill Valley and my father are forever; they live in another place—within my heart.

I sat down on my bench, and wrote a thank-you note.

Dear Dad,

Thank you for working hard so your kids could grow up in Mill Valley.

In the hushed redwood cathedral of Old Mill Park, Cascade Creek's cold, clear waters baptized me as I waded, my bare feet sinking into the soft gravel bottom. I hopped from stone to stone, climbed the boulders lining the creek side, and warmed myself in a random patch of sun.

I thought everybody grew up as I did under protective redwoods and enchanted fogs as deer grazed, silent, behind our home. I thought everyone's relatives visited to see where you lived. I never realized people from the world over visited Muir Woods to see the redwoods.

Now I find clarity, Dad, growing up under a mountain with bountiful springs amid lofty redwoods and open spaces that shielded me from the real world.

Thank you for meeting the challenge of raising kids during a cultural upheaval. Please accept my thanks for being such a dedicated father. And thank you for living in a materialistic society as a man of faith. I'm sorry I'm not Catholic anymore.

And thank you for Our Lady of Mount Carmel Church.

It's still standing.

I put down my pen, closed my eyes, and lifted my face to the sun's waning rays. I used to play under the redwoods as a kid; their blackened, scarred trunks from lightning strikes had made excellent witch houses. Well-adapted to surviving a wildfire's terrific damage, they were hard to kill, with their old growth—thick bark can withstand any assault. If flames consume a majestic crown or weaken a trunk so it topples onto the forest floor, the tree sprouts new growth at once. The tree's name, Sequoia sempervirens, means "always flourishing."

Dad's death forced me to grow up. I had rooted myself in the earth, always flourishing in the beauty of the present moment and living as nobly as a redwood reaching to the sky.

A girl stood among the horses grazing on Horse Hill.

A writer stood next to her on the red-bricked plaza.
And her father stood next to her.

35

EXPLODING VALENCIA

Abrupt explosions jolted us and rockets whistled past our heads. Amid the acrid scent of gunpowder mixed with fried churros, children threw sizzling firecrackers at our feet, giggling. Then came massive explosions that rocked the pavement under us as one hundred and ten pounds of gunpowder and four tons of dynamite vaporized in the central plaza.

Together with Rob, I reveled in this pyrotechnic chaos.

In Valencia, Spain, we had thrown ourselves into the weaponized silliness of the Las Fallas Festival, an anarchic celebration of creativity and rebirth. Once a pagan purification rite of spring, this madcap version of Burning Man had become a fusion of art, humor, and destruction. The trip had been Rob's idea. "I want to see everything blow up," he'd said, his enthusiasm infectious.

It was hard to argue with his excitement, though deep inside, I carried a different, heavier longing. I had toyed with the idea of returning to Perugia with Rob yet stayed silent. How could I explain to him my pull to the place where my life had shattered?

The years had dulled the sharp edges of my past, but the loss remained, buried and unhealed. However, since my moment of clarity in Mill Valley almost two years ago, my life had flowed smoothly. My father's exuberant love of life inspired me to seek joy, travel with Rob, and embrace the world instead of running from it. Still, Perugia lingered in the shadows of my soul.

I'd told myself Las Fallas was a safer choice—a wild, purging celebration far from what awaited in Italy. In Valencia's old Roman quarter, we wandered among the fallas—garish caricatures of pop culture icons or fairytale characters, many two stories high. Constructed of wood, cardboard, papier-mâché, and polystyrene, every falla, stuffed with fireworks and gunpowder, was astonishingly flammable.

A fifty-foot Moses loomed over the central plaza, commenting on Spain's banking crisis with his tablet emblazoned with the commandment "Thou shalt not steal."

After four days of insanity, a fiery finale arrived at nightfall; during the burning of the fallas, the cremà, seven hundred fallas were blown up around the old quarter. As the blazes sent a hellish glow into the sky, we dodged snaking fire hoses and waded through paper shards of exploded firecrackers. At one in the morning, we joined the crowds in the central plaza for the incendiary climax, which would include bombs detonating inside the giant Moses.

Men on ladders lit ropes laced with firecrackers, causing sparking explosions to race toward the giant falla. A swift hellfire soon engulfed Moses, his eyes glowing red as his insides burst into flames.

I climbed a light pole for a better view. From my perch, I yelled down to Rob, "I can feel the heat from up here."

Spellbound, he never responded.

In the inferno's warmth and illumination, flames licked at Moses, and I was struck with a thought: *Stealing is wrong, and what Gul stole still smolders inside me.*

My innocence.

My sense of safety.

My peace.

And the girl I used to be.

My overwhelming pull toward Perugia was a compulsion I couldn't ignore. Going back felt both essential and unbearable. Like running into a firestorm—painful yet cleansing—to illuminate the way forward in my healing.

I was no longer the girl who left Italy all those years ago, shattered and scared. I'd grown as a woman who wrestled with loss, built herself anew, and learned to stand again. Yet the echoes of my past still haunted me.

As giant Moses furiously burned, I wondered if I could incinerate my anger, my grief, my shame.

As if in answer, the misshapen, black structure of Moses collapsed into a heap of glowing debris, his destruction swift and absolute. The crowd's roar thundered as bulldozers fired up to shovel away the wreckage of ash and cinders.

Back in our hotel room, I drifted into a restless sleep amid the sounds of explosions.

By morning, Valencia had transformed, the streets quiet and clean. Children walked to school, birds trilled in the trees, and buses hummed down the avenues. Life moved on.

"Sometimes you have to blow everything up," I said to Rob over our coffees, more to myself than to him. "Then, you can find a sort of peace."

Rob smiled, oblivious to the weight of my words. For him, Las Fallas offered an extreme adventure. For me, Las Fallas offered a choice.

Healing never happens in the shadows—it demands light.

What if, in the place where everything had broken, I could reclaim my power and become lighter, freer?

What if, after all this time, I could go back to Perugia and fuse the fractured pieces of my past into something whole...and finally declare victory over Gul?

36

A GHOST IN PERUGIA

In the crush and rush of Roma Termini, we searched for our train to Perugia during a long march down a remote platform. Footsore and weary, I rolled my suitcase as sweat and apprehension soaked my body underneath my heavy sweater. After twenty minutes of walking down an endless platform, I wondered if I wasn't supposed to catch this train.

Finally, we found our train and a porter who settled us in a first-class compartment. As the train rolled away, I bent forward to stare out the window, wondering how I'd feel back in Perugia. Would it look the same? Smell the same?

I had booked our trip for a spring arrival to avoid the fierce cold. I wanted to experience the hill town under a warm sun, strolling down Corso Vannucci and creating happy memories with Rob. I wanted to visit the nearby village of Rob's grandfather, Sigillo, to explore his family history.

Rob said, "I'm excited to see Sigillo. And look at you! You left a poor student, and now you're coming back in first class."

"Yeah, we're staying at the same hotel where I stole toilet paper from the lobby restroom."

"Hey, did you see how the porter spoke Italian to me?" Rob asked. "They always speak Italian to me, Lenore, not you."

"This is Italy. They always speak to the man, and, well, you do look like an Italian."

This was true. Rob exuded a quiet confidence, his crisp new jeans, Italian wool bomber jacket, and curly hair giving him the air of a well-dressed Italian man. As I admired Rob's wardrobe, my thoughts betrayed me. They swung between my present and past on this train to Perugia, pulling me back to Gul, the man who had stolen from me. Another thought struck me like a sharp Umbrian wind, cold and uninvited. Gul had worn a well-cut overcoat—a thief in disguise—on the night we met in the piazza for dinner. A rapist wearing a mask, he stole what he had no right to take.

Yet today I traveled with my protector, my anchor, feeling the unshakable safety Rob had brought into my life. His love wrapped around me like armor. Alongside Rob, I deserved to live a life that totally belonged to me—safe, vibrant, and free.

If only I could reconcile my past and present, keeping them separate instead of bleeding into each other.

It's so hard to come back here.

"Look at that storm," said Rob.

"Looks like we're rolling into a big wall of black," I said. "At the end of April!"

Hailstones began an intense tapping on the roof; cocooned against the storm in our compartment, I couldn't talk to Rob about my emotions. If I mentioned my sad history, as usual, he'd feel too hurt to talk about it.

But what about me? Wasn't I the one all alone in a foreign country? Wasn't I the one forced to have sex? Wasn't I the one navigating the confusing complexity of rape as a teenager?

I leaned against the window, exhausted.

Speeding through Italy's lush, verdant center, we crossed a swollen Tiber River, and a sign for Perugia raced by.

"We're close," said Rob, my happy explorer. "You excited?"

I nodded, forcing a smile as cat claws scrambled my insides. Racing toward a night in my past I loathed to relive, the enormity of returning sank in. *Why am I pretending the dark thoughts roaming my mind don't exist? I've got to stop hiding them from Rob and tell him what's going on with me.*

Suburban apartment buildings swept by our window and our train slowed to a stop. I sank into my seat.

"Great, we're here," Rob said, grabbing our suitcases from the overhead rack.

Inwardly kicking myself, I pasted a smile on my face. "And I know exactly where we'll have dinner, at La Rosetta. You'll love it. Oh, and I want to show you my old school. And where I lived on Via Cartolari. All my old haunts."

In a hard rain, our cab climbed to the hill town's ancient center and the Hotel Brufani Palace, a five-star atop three-thousand-year-old Etruscan ruins. Rolling our bags through the cream-colored marble lobby, I jerked my head toward the ladies' restroom. "Over there," I whispered, "the scene of my petty theft."

Rob laughed.

In our room, French doors opened south to a classic Umbrian scene. Sharp green Italian cypresses pierced the sky, and church towers and roseate tiled roofs dotted the green hills tumbling away from our hotel. A thick fog overlaid these hillsides, and rain pelted the glass.

After dining at the delectable La Rosetta, back in our room, Rob beckoned me to bed. As I sunk into the fleeting reprieve of intimacy, trauma's emotional weight lifted away. There, in his arms, I could silence the voices. I could let the heat of his touch burn away the cold of Perugia. In a romantic Italy, this escape was effortless.

The next morning, we stepped into the rain pelting Corso Vannucci. The locals dressed in heavy arctic jackets, jeans, and boots, still displaying that Italian trick of looking excruciatingly chic. Surrounded by Italy's lyrical cadence, we dodged shallow, overflowing water channels carved centuries ago in the paving stones. Other things hadn't changed; college students still sat at umbrella tables outside the gelateria where I had discovered cinnamon gelato.

Strolling along the Corso, memories surfaced in jagged fragments like shards of broken glass catching the light. A familiar building caught the corner of my eye—the former site of the telephone office where I had once dialed home, sick and desperate. The scent of rain on cobblestones carried me back to the bus stop where Gul had met me that evening.

The enormity of revisiting my pain on purpose made my head spin. I craved a pack of Dunhill cigarettes and a glass of wine to numb the ache in my heart.

"Let's check out my old club," I said, feeling curious.

I led Rob through a labyrinth of narrow streets down to Via Sant'Agata. The street grates stank of musty water, a visceral reminder of the loneliness that drove me out of my room and into the club. The club was closed, but I peered through grimy windows, searching for a trace of what it had once been. Where elegant white banquettes and red walls once welcomed me in a haze of cigarette smoke, I now saw the décor of a British low-market pub.

It's gone—that sanctuary of the ghost of the girl.

In this place I had tried to dance away my pain. In this place I had begun my years of fleeing.

Why did I run so far, so intentionally, on so many adventures? Why did I throw myself into the whirling winds of life, wifedom, and motherhood, piling on the miles as if running could erase what had happened here?

It hadn't been just distance I craved—it was escape. Escape from the part of me that shattered that night. Escape from the stolen bit of innocence that corrupted what my future might have held.

No wonder my obsession with travel—writing about new places and creating new stories—became my refuge. Feeling in control, I rewrote the narrative and erased the original story I couldn't bear to face. Yet I realized no amount of distance or reinvention could undo what had been done.

The palpable enormity of this truth felt unbearable.

We walked in silence. Then, I said, "Let's go. I'll show you where I used to live."

At Via Cartolari, number 22, I looked up to the third story and happily pointed out to Rob the wooden window shutters outside my former room. I couldn't tell him that, while living there, I had hidden my rage and helplessness. There, I had convinced myself the rape wasn't a big deal, yet I sought escape, like a terrified dog running from bursting fireworks.

What was I expecting to find here?

"My face hurts," I said to Rob. "It's even too cold for a cinnamon gelato."

As we hiked uphill to the piazza, I was sweating under my clothing layers, my shoulders slumped, and a chill wind bit my cheeks.

The rain began to pound so we warmed up over coffee in an old hangout, Caffè Turreno. Holding my cup to warm my hands, I said, "It's hard to enjoy anything in this weather."

"We'll make the best of it," said Rob, ever positive. "We'll just dip in and out of cafés to get warm."

When the rain let up, I said, "Let's go see my old school."

I led Rob downhill on Via Ulisse Rocchi, past the butcher shop that had hung dead rabbits outside its door. Through the Etruscan Arch, we entered Piazza Fortebraccio where I pointed to the stately Palazzo Gallenga.

"There it is!" I said, quickening my pace toward the palazzo. I was about to re-enter the world that had ignited that adventurous girl who bounded up marble steps every morning, excited to learn Italian.

"Wow," Rob said. His eyes widened as he took in the grandeur. "It really is a palace. I thought you were exaggerating."

"Wait until you see Classroom Three," I said, smiling. "It's so elegant."

Reaching the massive entry doors, I grabbed one of the carved handles and pulled. It wouldn't open. I tried again, harder this time. Nothing. "What?" I muttered, yanking with all my strength. The door held fast.

I took a step back, my chest tightening as disbelief gave way to frustration. "Are we locked out? On a Monday?" Suddenly, I wasn't standing in front of my school anymore. I was nineteen again, wrestling with a bathroom door lock after I fled Gul's predatory gaze in the school café. That stuck door lock refused to release, leaving me trapped, powerless.

Rob pointed to a notice near the doorway. "What's that say?"

Grateful for a distraction, I leaned in to translate it. "Oh, it says its closed for National Liberation Day. It's a holiday commemorating the end of Nazi occupation and Fascism in Italy." Half-disappointed and half-relieved, I stepped farther from the door.

"Well, what's next?" asked Rob.

"What's next?" I echoed under my breath, the words bitter in my mouth. The weight of this moment felt heavier than the damp air, colder than the stones underfoot.

I turned away from my school with a bitterness biting and unrelenting. "Let's go back to the piazza," I said lightly, my words scraping my throat like sandpaper.

As we climbed a steep hill, I dragged my fingers along a rough stone wall. Its sharpness grated my skin, grounding me in the present, even as my mind spiraled into the past. I'd come here to unlock something—a sense of closure, a path to healing. Instead, the past had closed in, sealing me inside the very memories I'd hoped to abandon.

Perugia weighed on me now, pressing down like wet stones in my pockets. Each step grew heavier, the hope I'd brought with me slipping away.

Locked out again. From the school. From healing. From a life I believe I could reclaim.

But wasn't it always that way? Here, doors never opened easily for me. I had to pry them loose, break them down—or find another way through.

For now, though, I walked uphill in silence, shivering in the chill air.

In the piazza, we walked past the Palazzo dei Priori, Perugia's magistrate building. When I looked upward and spied the silent relics of Perugia's gory past, I froze.

37

SPIKES AND CAGES

I stared at the black iron spikes jutting skyward on the palazzo's tall wall facing Corso Vannucci. I had read about them in *The Story of Perugia,* an 1898 book by Margaret Symonds and Lina Duff Gordon. No guidebooks mentioned those spikes today.

During the medieval era, iron cages had swung from those spikes protruding above me, confining naked, starving prisoners to death. From the palazzo's beautiful arched windows, soldiers had run spears through the cages to detect if a criminal had become a corpse. If not, their blood dripped onto Corso Vannucci where their families grieved and the citizenry jeered.

Condemned women, stripped naked by soldiers, also hung in freezing cages. Among them were herbalists accused of inducing abortions, midwives convicted of witchcraft after a botched birth, or girls inconveniently impregnated after rape by powerful nobles.

My mind raced, caught in the jagged edges and ripped seams of my history, spinning endlessly, always returning to the same pain.

The notorious spikes jutting from between the tall, elegant windows of the Palazzo dei Priori.
© Lenore Greiner 2016.

I clenched my freezing, ungloved hands into fists. Perugia had impaled me once before, and here I was again, impaled anew—not by the town itself, but by the cycles within me that refused to break.

The locked door at my old school echoed in my mind as a cruel metaphor for the barriers I kept encountering. No matter how far I thought I'd traveled, I always circled back to this place of becoming stuck.

"Don't stay here," a voice inside whispered. "Get out. There's nothing here for you."

Perugia's spirit felt hostile, pushing me away, and I fell into an old pattern: escape. The urge to flee rose, sharp and insistent, but as I opened my mouth to tell Rob I wanted to leave—now, today—I stopped. If I asked him to leave without seeing his grandfather's town of Sigillo, I'd make this trip all about me when it was his trip, too.

As crowds swirled around us, my head swam, and a light-headed sensation of feeling trapped grew stronger.

"Let's walk on," I said, grabbing Rob's hand and pulling him down the Corso, moving quickly, needing the safety of our hotel. My legs felt like they couldn't move fast enough. I wasn't walking around Perugia; I was running from the storm of my own memories circling within me.

As we neared the Giardini Carducci, the cold seeped into my bones as if the city itself were trying to root me in place. Rob paused at the overlook and wrapped his arm around me, his warmth anchoring me against the cold. I leaned into him, desperate for stability, and the tightness in my chest loosened a bit.

"Beautiful valley," he said, gazing across the Spoleto Valley toward Assisi, where Saint Francis was born.

I managed a watery smile but stayed silent. Below our feet lay Etruscan ruins where Saint Francis himself had been imprisoned during Assisi's war with Perugia. A year later, the saint had returned home to search for healing through spirituality. I knew my own cycles of grief and trauma were far from divine, and I was nowhere near beatification.

Charcoal clouds rolled across the sky, heavy with rain, mirroring my emotions.

"If only I could cry," I whispered, more to myself than to Rob.

Did I need to keep running through the rain and cold, through icy puddles and slippery stones? I knew the circles would continue, replaying the nonlinear paths of grief and trauma twisting inside me like a labyrinth. But I also knew that healing never runs in a straight line; it spirals. The only way out was through—round and round—until something new could appear.

That evening, a gruff restaurateur grudgingly seated us for dinner, slamming menus onto the table as if we were a great inconvenience. While dining on Umbrian cuisine, Rob's fork clattered onto his plate. "These greens! They taste like grass," he said, gesturing at what looked like sautéed lawn clippings alongside a tender slice of Umbrian pork.

"That can't be right." I took a tentative bite, and my senses bloomed with the scent of freshly mown spring lawns.

"Oh my God, you're right!" I emptied my mouth into a snowy white napkin. Laughing, I said, "Looks the prankster of UC Davis just got pranked by a pissed-off restaurateur."

Rob chuckled and then suddenly turned serious. "Let's leave Perugia tomorrow."

"What?" For a moment, I felt buoyant with joy until guilt slammed into me. "But don't you want to visit Sigillo?"

"No," Rob replied, his gaze far away. "When I saw those round green hills across the valley today, they looked just like San Jose's foothills. And I thought, no wonder my family settled there. They knew good tomato-growing land when they saw it."

"Yes! Let's end this magical misery tour," I said, relieved. "I can't stay here any longer, Rob. It's too hard. You know . . . all my memories."

"Okay," he said softly.

I wanted to voice how walking these streets twisted a knife into my old wounds, but I stopped myself. With piercing clarity, a truth cut deep: all these years—first with Dad, now with Rob—in a misguided act of self-sacrifice, I had shouldered their pain. I shielded the men I loved from my harsh reality and paid the price with pieces of myself.

Resentment burned low and steady inside me, but I resigned myself to letting go.

We rushed back to our hotel and booked a morning train south to the sun, to Ostuni, my grandfather's village on the heel of Italy's stiletto boot. In our room, I packed my suitcase as my shoulders and body loosened and my tension ebbed.

The next morning, our rapido, or fast train, raced down the Adriatic seacoast to Apulia, a province foreigners rarely visited. Outside our window, the gem-like waters of the Adriatic and Ionian Seas merged, as blue as the Caribbean.

"I bet it's getting warmer the more south we go," said Rob.

I relaxed in my comfortable seat, facing our table laden with my journal, a bottle of mineral water, and snacks. *Wow, that was some Italian Liberation Day!* I thought. *Liberating myself from those cages and spikes.*

A crazy notion hit me: I had never *wanted* to let go of my trauma. I held onto it like a talisman, a piece of my identity impossible to release. I never needed to return to Perugia to heal from my imprisonment. I needed to free myself from my *need* to live in pain.

I no longer needed to carry the unbearable weight of silence alone. Freeing myself never required mere solitary reflections scrawled into my journal. My freedom required digging deep down for self-compassion, vulnerability, and the strength to ask Rob for what I needed.

So I promised myself I would try. Try to speak. Try to trust. Try to show Rob the woman he loved and to share my darkest thoughts and every piece of me I had hidden away.

As our train raced away from iron cages, locked doors, and dead ends hidden behind heartbreaking beauty, I gazed at the brilliant blue sea glowing under the sun outside my window. With the same clarity of those waters, I realized coming to Perugia had been a good idea—it illuminated my path forward.

I held up my past to the gilded sunlight bathing the wet stones and watched it dissolve into a literal renaissance, a rebirth. I had just freed myself by literally moving forward and riding away on this train. *Not* escaping.

The real tragedy isn't my need to escape, but the wound forcing me to flee in the first place.

Inside, I felt a wisp of a smile from the ghost of the girl.

38

SOUTH TO OSTUNI

In a gathering dusk, we disembarked from our train in Ostuni, the White City, the birthplace of my grandfather Joe. After we caught a taxi, we drove past the old quarter, which resembled a whitewashed Greek village. Known as the "Wedding Cake," it glowed against an indigo sky just like it had when I visited after my spring break years ago.

Heading to a historical artifact from my paternal history, a fortified farm called a masseria, our taxi flew past olive orchards down narrow roads lined with rock walls.

While enduring bloody invasions by the Byzantines, Normans, Spanish, and Turks, my paternal ancestors had built these fortress-farms throughout the countryside. Across centuries of invasions, these walled compounds ensured survival by sheltering people, animals, and food.

Exhausted, hungry, and way past dinnertime, we halted at the gate of our agritourism inn, the Masseria Il Frantoio, for a week's stay. We walked through an arch underneath the sigil of the Tanzarella family who built this masseria in the early 1500s. Within the white walls, we crossed a travertine courtyard past a family chapel. In the dim, our hostess appeared.

"Come," she said, ushering us inside a former animal shed, now an empty restaurant. Under low, vaulted ceilings, before a raging fire, we sat at a candlelit table set for two where place cards displayed our names in calligraphy. I sank into my soft chair, which glowed in the firelight, overwhelmed by this dreamlike welcome, surreal in its hospitality.

"We have prepared a snack for you," said our hostess.

Rob leaned toward me and whispered, "Hopefully without lawn clippings."

A side table held bottles of wine, mineral water, the house olive oil, and small dishes of farm-grown almonds and olives. Our hostess served platters of tomato rolls, lasagna, freshly baked bread, salad, and homemade salami adorned with wildflowers.

Then, she gestured to a tray.

Dessert.

Yes, our lovely "snack" included a ricotta cake for two, lying daintily in a pool of Chantilly cream. In the candlelight, we smiled at our good fortune.

Afterward, our hostess checked us into our room, a converted storehouse with vaulted ceilings and high windows. She lifted a rug laid over a creaky wooden door in the floor to reveal a secret storeroom where the Tanzarellas had hidden grain during all the sackings.

Feeling exhausted yet nurtured, I lay my head down in our big bed underneath a thick duvet and slept deeply in the quiet of the countryside.

In the morning, we explored the estate on a brilliant spring day. We exited the courtyard through a Moorish arch and entered a limonaia, a walled citrus grove irrigated Arab-style with stone water channels. Beyond the masseria walls, under a clear sky, we crossed a meadow dotted with two-thousand-year-old olive trees. Each bore a metal ID tag and a name: Sofia, Giuseppe, Sandro. Considered living history, these gnarled ancients were cared for and preserved by the Italian government.

"Rob, these trees were alive when Jesus walked the earth. Look, they still bear fruit after two millennia."

"That's amazing."

Over time, each trunk of a two-thousand-year-old olive tree split into two and twisted into a double helix shape like a strand of DNA.

"My ancestors may have planted these trees," I said. "And nurtured them for the olive oil."

We hiked past white pear and carob trees, wild berries and wild-flowers, as spring bloomed in the fecund soil. As birds sang, we walked past rows of spring onions, herbs, and strawberries, all grown for the masseria restaurant.

With each crunch of my feet on the gravel road, my steps became lighter and more energetic. Everything about this land felt welcoming, alive, and warm.

We found a trace of an old Roman road traversing the olive groves, terraced with native stone walls. I hopped atop a wall and studied the blue Adriatic beyond, the air redolent of the sea.

"This is some hardscrabble land," I said. "You can't grow tomatoes here. You can't run cattle. Only olive trees thrive here."

"And for thousands of years," said Rob.

"Yeah. God, it's so beautiful here. Yet my grandfather never talked about Ostuni. And if he did, it was never with nostalgia. I guess because of the crushing poverty; it's called 'miseria' in Italian."

Desperate with hunger, my ancestors foraged wild onions, wild asparagus, and another weed that gained fame as arugula. Seafood came from the Adriatic. If fishermen sailed back in empty boats, their wives cooked a seaweed soup called the "soup of the escaped fish."

Walking on, I said, "Let's make no plans for the rest of our week here."

"Good idea. We'll just do whatever we want, day by day."

Every morning, we hiked in the countryside, and every afternoon, we explored the "Wedding Cake" and dined on regional cuisine. At night, I slept soundly within the sanctuary of our fortified farm. Surrounded by thick walls and heavy gates, I understood the profound relief of true safety, a stillness quieting the instinct to constantly fight for survival. Safety isn't just a shield, it's the foundation of living authentically in order to truly flourish.

One afternoon, over plates of black ink orecchiette pasta, Rob said, "You're very quiet."

I leaned back in my chair, stretched, and exhaled. "I am calm. This is the Italy I longed for."

Between sips of local white wine, I explained how I found in Italy escape and entrapment. "It's both a sanctuary and a labyrinth for me," I said. "While visiting as an adult, I always danced between a sunny Italy in Orvieto with my family or in lovely Venice with you. But this time, stone-cold Perugia was no fun at all."

"Well, the more you come here and have fun like everyone else, the more you can leave the bad behind," said Rob.

His flippant response angered me; I wanted to tell him how rough Perugia was on me. Or just talk about what had happened to me there. But I kept quiet. A surge of frustration and helplessness ran through my body.

We finished our lunch to walk around as my head drooped in defeat.

At breakfast the next morning, a British guest told us, "Oh, you must go to Otranto. It has a lovely Roman port and the best seafood restaurants."

We looked at each other and smiled. "Let's go," said Rob.

We rented a little Fiat 500 and drove south to Otranto. During our drive, Rob asked, "What are you writing about?"

I put down my journal. "I'm writing about how the local dishes seem more Middle Eastern than Italian. Like lamb spit-roasted over a fire or served with poppy leaves. And fish with raisins, pistachios with orange honey, or saffron-infused goat cheese."

"Interesting, it could be," said Rob, eyes on the road.

"Oh, I just remembered something. My grandfather used to tell us that, though we're one hundred percent Italian, we might have some Greek or Turkish blood because of invasions. Maybe that explains the cuisine."

In seaside Otranto, our hunger led us to a restaurant terrace overlooking a pretty fishing marina. We ordered a seafood platter—fresh, crisp, alive with flavor. Between bites, I read Otranto's history aloud to Rob, a history buried in blood and shame.

"In 1480, a Turkish fleet invaded the port town. Over fifteen thousand Turkish soldiers decapitated the men and killed every child. They raped the women, an act of humiliation to break their spirits. For over a year, the Turks ran raids up the coast until routed out—" I stopped.

I looked into Rob's eyes; he saw the connection before I even voiced it—my own ordeal at the hands of a Turk in modern-day Italy.

I whispered, "They never stood a chance. Just like me." I couldn't stay quiet any longer.

He took a swallow of his beer. "Yeah."

"Oh my God, maybe those Turks raped my ancestors. My grandfather said that we could have Turkish blood. Am I descended from those women? And the Turks who . . . hurt them?"

I took a gulp of my white wine. "Rob, didn't you see what I was going through in Perugia? Because of what had happened to me there?"

He stiffened. "Well, you didn't seem happy to be there at all, but I never put two and two together. Even though you were acting cold and distant, not your usual bubbly self."

"Oh," I said, seeing sadness in his eyes.

"I knew you wanted to leave right away because you kept saying, 'It's so cold here. I forgot how cold it gets here.'"

He gazed out to sea. "My intent was to see where my grandfather came from," he said. "And I was so pleased that you wanted to show me around Perugia. But I couldn't talk about the bad times, and I didn't think that you could either."

"So, how come we can *never* talk about it, about the rape?"

"It's a subject I just can't—it's totally impossible for me. It hurts too much."

"But shouldn't the person I love more than anyone in the whole world be the one I *can* talk to?"

"You need my support," he answered. "But if I fell apart while talking about it, then I couldn't support you."

He drained the rest of his beer.

Then it hit me—Rob was Gul's victim as well.

The weight of understanding this crushed me. As sorrow and shock cascaded through me, I saw him in a new light. Rob wasn't just my rock; he had been weathering his own storm all along, enduring so much while trying to protect me.

And I understood all too well his instinct to stay silent. I could see my own reflection in his silence. While I believed silence was keeping me imprisoned, he believed silence was the way to break free.

We had both been forced to bury our pain.

He went on, saying, "You know, I always felt bad about how I wasn't strong enough when I was sick with cancer. How I couldn't support you. That whole experience pushed you to your limit. Little babies in the house and all."

Like me, Rob was a survivor of trauma, bearing his own invisible wounds. He knew how painful memories could dominate your thoughts and rob you of energy, making the struggle to survive even more difficult.

This was never just my tragedy—it's always been ours.

A new silence stretched between us. This time, the weight of my ancestors—those who survived and those who hadn't—filled the stillness.

I could see them clearly and understand them deeply. The trauma those women had suffered—psychologically and physically—had lasting effects on their memory as well as the cultural fabric. The toll of the Turkish massacres, sexual violence, and occupation created lives of constant fear. With an unfathomable fortitude, my ancestors had survived the Turkish occupation inside the fortress farms they constructed around the countryside.

Dad's father, my grandfather Joe, had inherited their fortitude as well. Living with never-ending poverty, at seventeen he had abandoned his roots for a safe, prosperous future in a new land.

Was I led on that impulsive trip to Otranto to discover this history? Perhaps we all end up where we need to be to learn the meaning of the cycles within our lives and across generations.

After this revelation, I reflected on what my ancestors were teaching me. Their story symbolized the reclamation of my own life after trauma, though scars remained.

I no longer felt like a victim but connected—connected to a lineage of survivors.

The pain Gul had inflicted lived in the past; he had stolen a piece of me, but he could never steal my present or future. The life I lived now, alongside Rob, was mine—safe, vibrant, and free.

I once believed my trauma defined me, and I lived as if it did. In truth, my past, as painful as it was, had never defined me.

What did define me was my inheritance from my ancestors, their strength and resilience.

They had survived sackings and sieges.

I had survived my own.

My ancestral DNA encompassed it all, woven into a double helix just like the trunks of the two-thousand-year-old olive trees thriving in stony, unforgiving soil.

After our afternoon meal, we descended from the restaurant, strolled along the waterside in the historic center, and stopped at the ramparts above the harbor.

Rob took my hand, grounding me just as he always had. "You're stronger than anyone will ever know," he said, his voice gentle. "You've come a long way."

"I think so, too." My healing journey never ran in a straight line but careened on a messy, complicated journey. I had always hidden my shadow—the darker, more chaotic parts of me. Escaping or hiding never truly protected me; it only kept me stuck. The survival strategies I clung to as a teenager had no place in my life.

From the height of the ramparts, we watched the sun split the afternoon clouds and shimmer its rays upon the ocean. The air shifted around me, and I let everything wash away—the pain, the shame, the anger.

I stood bathed in a new light. Buoyant with happiness, I asked Rob, "Ready to head back?"

Still traveling together today, Rob and I wander through a Marrakech market.
© Lenore Greiner 2022.

"Yeah. Let's go."

Our tiny Fiat flew past green farmer fields of durum wheat, grown for pasta flour, and spring wildflowers dotting the nurturing countryside.

Inside, the ghost of the girl smiled, no longer knocking at my conscience, demanding my attention.

For the first time I saw Italy clearly. The past lived in Italy—it would always live there. It no longer held me prisoner, locked inside an iron cage. My ancestors had gifted me what I had been searching for: the sense that I could carry the weight of my past without letting it break me.

Gul's force in my life had diminished; he was just a criminal who escaped justice. Though the pain he had inflicted was real, I now knew I could safely condemn it—and him—to the past, where shadows belong.

As our little car raced northward, a radiant Italy stretched before me, the adventurous girl who once dreamed of becoming a writer fully alive—she had never really left me. And I had never really abandoned her. Together, we had survived.

The Beginning

ACKNOWLEDGMENTS

Writing a memoir resembles a protracted childbirth, as painful and joyful as bringing a baby into the world but with tons more kicking and screaming.

I have a massive appreciation for those wonderful souls who helped me, or even dragged me, down my memoir-writing path. If I've forgotten to thank anyone, know that, as you read this, I'm kicking myself.

To Don George, co-founder and chairman of the Book Passage Travel Writers and Photographers Conference, a big thank you for sharing his love of travel writing and creating four days of magic for travel writers, both celebrated and aspiring. And much gratitude to Kathryn Petrocelli, owner of the Book Passage bookstore in Corte Madera, CA, for valiantly corralling our tribe without a hitch every August.

I'm indebted to one conference faculty member, Larry Habegger, who introduced me to the fine craft of memoir writing and illuminated my path toward publishing this book. With infinite patience, Larry edited and counseled me while I talked too much. Everything worked out though because, thanks to Larry, this book was born at Book Passage.

I'm forever grateful to Chris Reynolds for our rich conversations about travel journalism or simply about all the awesome places to explore. He knows so much about everything in the world, and the *Los Angeles Times* is fortunate indeed to publish his byline.

Thank you to Tim Cahill, the Chuck Yeager of adventure travel writing, who accepted me into his Book Passage writing intensive one year.

As I distilled his creativity, humanity, and humor, he encouraged my work, causing me to dance upon clouds for weeks.

At several turning points, the accomplished writer, Judy Reeves, always offered key advice in answer to my rambling queries. You are as true a teacher and mentor as you are an excellent writer.

I want to thank my gifted, sharp-eyed editor, Leslie Ferguson, who has my undying gratitude and awe. Leslie's masterful editing resulted in a better memoir while preserving the heart of my book. Without her clever insights, vast expertise, and wise words, this book would've been twice as long and half as coherent. To Holly Kammier, Acorn Publishing's co-founder and Acquisitions Editor, thank you for your professionalism and for the opportunity to write my book with the creative freedom I craved.

Thanks to Kristen Fogle, the fearless director of San Diego Writers, Ink, whose programs and events gave me access to the vast writing community so integral to my work. And much gratitude to Tracy Jones, President of the International Memoir Writers Association, for her boundless enthusiasm about my work and publishing my stories in three *Shaking the Tree* memoir anthologies. You are a treasure. To Marni Freedman, thanks for your writing advice, including these words, "Great job! Now go back and try again."

Writing is a solitary act, but without my writer's group—who understand my deep agony of getting it right—I would have lost my mind. Or at least my will to finish. Caroline, Janet, Helga, NancyPants, Nancy O., Heather, Paul, Susan, David, and Valerie, extraordinary writers all, you are my North Stars.

Personally speaking, I'm so lucky to have precious lifelong friends, including Elke, Nora, and LeeAnn. You have my immense gratitude for your ancient recollections, both foggy and distinct, during our walks down rugged memory lanes. To LeeAnn, your input after reading my manuscript made my heart soar, more meaningful because we've known each other since we were little. To Elke, my friend since toddlerhood, you're the rare "sister from another mother" who listened as I pondered my most profound spiritual questions. And to Nora, you make me laugh so much and your travel advice about Belize sent me on an exquisite journey of discovery. Grazie, bella! To Jackson and my sister, thank you for patiently answering my unending questions about Marin County life during the seventies as I taxed your decades-old memories.

To my wonderful, wild, and exceptional family—including those brave enough to marry into our crazy clan—thank you for the laughter and the love: Julie, Ralph, Phil, Joe, Mimi, Jim, Georgia, Carrie, Ray, Ronan, Luca, Teagan, Victoria, Michael, Kathy, Chloe, Nicolette, Levi, Emma, Matt, Maia, and Marco. Though some of us had questionable childhood adventures (yes, I'm talking about stealing candy from Mill Valley supermarkets), we all carry within us Dad's love, humor, and ability to make life an adventure.

To Rob, you made a sad girl laugh again and then devoted your life to her. Too young when we first met, I can't believe my dumb luck in landing my perfect partner in crime. We've endured the unendurable together, built a life rich in love together, and raised two beautiful children together. Over the years, you watched me grow as a writer and always supported me. Most of all, thank you for comforting me after too many hard days of writing and reliving unbearable memories—this book is just as much your accomplishment as it is mine.

ABOUT THE AUTHOR

Award-winning travel writer Lenore Greiner grew up in Marin County, where, at thirteen, she began her writing journey as a lifelong journal keeper.

At seventeen, she took off for Mexico to practice Spanish. At nineteen, her passion for adventure led her to Italy's heart to study Italian at the University for Foreigners in Perugia and immerse herself in art and culture.

There, the seeds of her memoir were sown.

Lenore has garnered eight prestigious Solas Awards for Best Travel Writing, and was honored in *Best American Travel Writing 2013*, edited by Elizabeth Gilbert. Her writing credits include *The New York Times*, *Newsday*, *San Francisco Chronicle*, *Delta Sky* in-flight, *Air New Zealand*, Fodor's Travel Publications, and three volumes of the anthology *Shaking the Tree*, curated by the International Memoir Writers Association.

A graduate of UC Davis, Lenore married her college sweetheart, and they now call Southern California home. They share two kids, two kayaks, and too many rambunctious grandkids.

www.ingramcontent.com/pod-product-compliance
Lightning Source LLC
Chambersburg PA
CBHW021711120626
46545CB00004B/1509